Local Economy

Linguistic Inquiry Monographs
Samuel Jay Keyser, general editor

Local Economy   Chris Collins

The MIT Press
Cambridge, Massachusetts
London, England

Set in Times Roman and Times Phonetic by The MIT Press.
Printed and bound in the United States of America.

Library of Congress Cataloging-in-Publication Data

Collins, Chris, 1963–
    Local economy / Chris Collins.
        p.   cm. — (Linguistic inquiry monographs ; 29)
    Includes bibliographical references and index.
    ISBN 0-262-03242-2 (alk. paper). — ISBN 0-262-53144-5 (pbk. : alk. paper)
    1. Grammar, Comparative and general–Syntax. 2. Generative grammar. 3. Minimalist theory (Linguistics)   I. Title.   II. Series.
P291.C57   1996
415—dc20   96-8711
                                                                                                    CIP

Contents

Series Foreword

We are pleased to present the twenty-ninth in the series *Linguistic Inquiry Monographs*. These monographs present new and original research beyond the scope of the article. We hope they will benefit our field by bringing to it perspectives that will stimulate further research and insight.

Originally published in limited editions, the *Linguistic Inquiry Monographs* are now more widely available. This change is due to the great interest engendered by the series and by the needs of a growing readership. The editors thank the readers for their support and welcome suggestions about future directions for the series.

Samuel Jay Keyser
for the Editorial Board

Acknowledgements

I would especially like to thank Noam Chomsky, Hiroyuki Ura, and Akira Watanabe for many interesting discussions on economy of derivation. Without them, I would not have been able to write this book.

Chapter 3 is a development and rethinking of collaborative work done with Phil Branigan on quotative inversion. The discussion of double object constructions in chapter 3 is based partly on collaborative work with Hoski Thráinsson.

Eun Cho, Molly Diesing, Hiroyuki Ura, Akira Watanabe, and Magui Suñer all read the original manuscript and provided me with very helpful comments.

Most of the material in this book has been developed considerably during seminars that I have given at Cornell University. In particular, the main ideas of chapters 4 and 5 originated in a workshop on phrase structure taught (with John Whitman) during the summer of 1994. In addition, portions of this book were presented at New York University in February 1995 and at the University of Connecticut in November 1995. I would like to thank Mark Baltin, Željko Bošković, Howard Lasnik, and all the other participants in these seminars and lectures for their interesting comments.

Lastly and most importantly, I would like to thank my family, Essi, Betty, and Atsufe, for putting up with me during the writing of this book.

Local Economy

Chapter 1

Introduction

In any theory of grammar, there will be three essential components: a lexicon, an interface with the mechanisms of production and perception (PF), and an interface with the interpretational system of semantics (LF). Given the physical parameters of the human experience, these components are a necessity on any theory of grammar.

A traditional way to relate these components (PF, LF, lexicon) in generative theory is through a derivation. Since LF and PF representations are composed of items drawn from the lexicon, it is natural to assume that the derivation takes items from the lexicon and combines them in certain ways.

Noam Chomsky (1991) postulated that this grammatical derivation is constrained by economy conditions, requiring that derivations be minimal. Under these conditions, if one derivation is shorter than another, the shorter blocks the longer, and the PF and LF corresponding to the blocked derivation are interpreted as unacceptable.

Given the three essential components of grammar (LF, PF and lexicon), and a derivational relationship between them constrained by economy, it is clear that one of the most important questions of syntax is what the economy conditions are. This has been the subject of many liberating studies, questioning every aspect of syntactic theory and trying to put the basic assumptions of syntactic theory on a more solid foundation.

In this book, I will propose that economy conditions are local, in a sense to be made specific. I will show how definite empirical consequences follow from this proposal. In particular, the fact that both locative and quotative inversion are allowed is a strong argument for local economy. In addition, I will show how a local perspective on economy has deep and far-reaching consequences for other areas of syntax.

There is a close relationship between the work presented in this book and that presented in the collected papers of Chomsky (1995). Many of the ideas in this book were developed as reactions to Chomsky's 1994 paper "Bare Phrase

Structure." Most of the analyses in this book were originally developed in the general framework of that paper and Chomsky's 1993 paper "A Minimalist Program for Linguistic Theory." Therefore, I will try to make clear at each point what my working assumptions are, and in what way I am departing from Chomsky's conclusions in his various papers. Although I will present definitions as needed, I will assume that the reader is familiar with Rizzi 1990 and Chomsky 1995. To restate all the arguments found in these two works would extend this book greatly.[1]

1.1 Definition of Local Economy

In order to define local economy, we must be more explicit about what a derivation is. Initially, I will follow Chomsky (1994, 1995) in my assumptions about the nature of derivations. Recall that any theory of syntax must contain a lexicon, a PF interface, and an LF interface. The interface with the lexicon is accomplished through the Numeration. The Numeration is defined as a set of pairs (LI, i), where LI is a lexical item and i is the index that tells how many times LI is to be selected from the Numeration. An element LI is selected (the operation Select) from the Numeration (reducing its index by one). In chapters 4 and 6, I will show how the concept of Numeration is not needed.

Given the Numeration, syntactic operations construct syntactic objects. Each of these objects roughly corresponds to a traditional phrase structure. The set of syntactic objects formed at a particular step in the derivation is $\Sigma = \{SO_1, SO_2, \ldots, SO_n\}$.

At each step, any one of the following syntactic operations can apply: Select, Merge, Move, Delete. Select selects a lexical item from the Numeration, reduces its index by one, and adds it to the set of syntactic objects Σ. Merge takes a pair of syntactic objects (SO_i, SO_j) and replaces them by a new object SO_k. I discuss the definition of the object formed by Merge in chapter 4. For now, I will write it simply $SO_k = \{SO_i, SO_j\}$. According to Chomsky (1995: 226), Merge and Select are not subject to economy conditions; these operations are costless. In chapter 4, I argue (*contra* Chomsky) that Merge is subject to economy conditions.

Move is simply defined as a sequence of the operations: Copy + Merge (see Chomsky 1995: 250 for a slightly different approach; see Kitahara 1994 for a related approach).[2] Copy takes any constituent and produces an identical copy which is added to Σ. I will assume that Copy is a reflex of Merge, in that it never occurs independently of Merge. Given this formulation, any constraints on Merge should also be constraints on Move. I come back to this in chapter 4.

One further stipulation is that Move must form a chain $(\alpha, t(\alpha))$, where $t(\alpha)$ is the trace of α.[3] I will refer to cases of Merge that are not part of Move as "pure Merge." For notional convenience, I will often simply write traces, where the copy theory of movement is not at issue.

Chomsky (1995: 253) argues that Move must meet several conditions as part of its definition. These include c-command, uniformity, Last Resort, and the Minimal Link Condition. I do not make these assumptions, as I will discuss at length in chapter 2.

For present purposes, I assume that Delete marks a constituent or a feature as not visible at the interface and not accessible to any further computations. Deletion is used in two places. First, features may undergo deletion if they enter into a checking relation. Second, features in one part of a chain may undergo deletion if identical to features in another part of the chain.

Given the operations above, each stage of the derivation is characterized by a set of syntactic objects Σ and the remaining part of the Numeration N. The operations above apply to this set Σ and the Numeration to form a new set Σ' and a modified Numeration N'. At some point in the derivation Σ, there is an operation Spell-Out that applies to Σ and starts the computation to PF.

In order to illustrate this system, consider the derivation of sentence (1).

(1)
The girl left.

The Numeration for this sentence is

N = {(the, 1), (girl, 1), (left, 1), (T, 1)}.

There are initially no formed syntactic objects. The complete derivation is shown in (2). (I will not usually go through derivations in this way.)

(2)

a.	N = {(the, 1), (girl, 1), (left, 1), (T, 1)} $\Sigma = \varnothing$
b. Select girl	N = {(the, 1), (girl, 0), (left, 1), (T, 1)} $\Sigma = \{girl\}$
c. Select the	N = {(the, 0), (girl, 0), (left, 1), (T, 1)} $\Sigma = \{girl, the\}$
d. Merge (girl, the)	N = {(the, 0), (girl, 0), (left, 1), (T, 1)} $\Sigma = \{\{girl, the\}\}$
e. Select left	N = {(the, 0), (girl, 0), (left, 0), (T, 1)} $\Sigma = \{\{girl, the\}, left\}$
f. Merge({girl, the}, left)	N = {(the, 0), (girl, 0), (left, 0), (T, 1)} $\Sigma = \{\{\{girl, the\}, left\}\}$

g. Select T $N = \{(\text{the}, 0), (\text{girl}, 0), (\text{left}, 0), (T, 0)\}$
                                                      $\Sigma = \{T, \{\{\text{girl}, \text{the}\}, \text{left}\}\}$

h. Merge $(T, \{\{\text{girl}, \text{the}\}, \text{left}\})$ $N = \{(\text{the}, 0), (\text{girl}, 0), (\text{left}, 0), (T, 0)\}$
                                                      $\Sigma = \{\{T, \{\{\text{girl}, \text{the}\}, \text{left}\}\}\}$

i. Copy $\{\text{girl}, \text{the}\}$ $N = \{(\text{the}, 0), (\text{girl}, 0), (\text{left}, 0), (T, 0)\}$
                                                      $\Sigma = \{\{\text{girl}, \text{the}\}, \{T, \{\{\text{girl}, \text{the}\}, \text{left}\}\}\}$

j. Merge $(\{\text{girl}, \text{the}\}, \{T, \{\{\text{girl}, \text{the}\}, \text{left}\}\})$

                                                      $N = \{(\text{the}, 0), (\text{girl}, 0), (\text{left}, 0), (T, 0)\}$
                                                      $\Sigma = \{\{\{\text{girl}, \text{the}\}, \{T, \{\{\text{girl}, \text{the}\}, \text{left}\}\}\}\}$

A condition on well-formed derivations is that by LF the Numeration must be exhausted and the set Σ must have only one element.

Given this much background, we can now define local economy as in (3).

(3)
Given a set of syntactic objects Σ which is part of derivation D,[4] the decision about whether an operation OP may apply to Σ (as part of an optimal derivation[5]) is made only on the basis of information[6] available in Σ.

This definition is very abstract, but it is based on a very simple intuition. During a derivation, at any step the decision about whether to apply an operation (in an optimal derivation) is based on the syntactic objects to which the operation is applying. In other words, the decision about whether to apply OP may not refer to another set of syntactic objects Σ' that is in D, or to what happens at LF and PF, nor to another set of syntactic objects Σ' that is in another derivation D'.

Perhaps the best way to grasp the definition of local economy is to compare it with one particular form of global economy, given in (4). (Here I follow Kitahara's (1995) convenient formulation.)

(4)   *Shortest Derivation Requirement (SDR)*
Minimize the number of operations necessary for convergence.

This definition is global in two very different ways. First, in order to decide whether an operation OP applying to a set Σ is in the optimal derivation, we must evaluate the number of steps in other derivations. This kind of comparison clearly does not fall under local economy. Note that in order to make this definition work, there must be some way of comparing derivations. A number of different approaches have been tried. For example, Collins (1994a) and Kitahara (1995) suggest that the two derivations must have the same LF objects. Chomsky (1994, 1995) assumes that two derivations are comparable if they have the same Numeration. In Chomsky's (1995: 227) terminology, the Numeration determines the reference set, and the only derivations that are considered are ones with the same Numeration.[7]

The other way in which this definition is global is that it involves a reference to the notion of convergence. A derivation is convergent if it leads to representations at PF and LF that satisfy Full Interpretation (FI). Minimally, a representation at PF satisfies FI only if all the strong features have been deleted. A representation at LF satisfies FI only if all the uninterpretable features have been deleted.[8] Crucially, in order to know if a derivation is convergent, it is necessary to verify the status of the final LF and PF representations of the derivation. This entails that (4) is not a local economy condition. In order to decide whether an operation OP applying to a set Σ is in the optimal derivation, we must verify that the derivation D (of which OP is an operation) leads to LF and PF representations satisfying Full Interpretation. This decision clearly does not conform to the definition of local economy.[9]

The definition of SDR in (4) is global in two ways: it refers to the number of steps in an alternative derivation and it refers to convergence. As we will see in this book, most of the global economy conditions that have been presented in the literature have these properties.

There are a number of reasons why local economy is superior to global economy. First, it is empirically superior, as the analyses of inversion in chapters 2 and 3 will show. Second, it tends to allow a more natural analysis of optionality, as will be discussed in section 1.3. Third, as was originally pointed out to me by Akira Watanabe, if global economy chooses the derivation with fewest steps, this is a case where the grammar is able to count. To evaluate the SDR, the number of operations in two different derivations must be counted and compared. This kind of comparison does not seem to be necessary in other parts of the grammar. For example, there is no condition that makes reference to the checking of exactly three features, or to comparing the number of violations of some condition against the number of violations of some other condition, or whatever.[10] What the grammar appears to be able to do is verify whether some simple condition (such as Last Resort or Minimality, as they are defined below) holds.

Perhaps the strongest reason to adopt local economy is that it places a strong constraint on possible economy conditions. This sharply limits the theoretical possibilities in giving an economy analysis of any particular phenomenon, which is desirable. Note that there is no question of learnability or explanatory adequacy. Whether or not local economy is adopted, the economy conditions are part of UG and therefore do not have to be acquired. [11]

1.2   Are the Economy Conditions Local?

In this section I survey some economy conditions proposed by several authors
and evaluate them as to whether they are local. As I will show, many if not
most of the recently proposed analyses that involve economy are global. Therefore,
it is not immediately obvious that economy conditions are defined locally, as I
propose they are.

I will start by reviewing some of the core cases of economy from Chomsky
and Lasnik 1993, Chomsky 1993, and Chomsky 1994. Let me start with the
definition of Greed given in Chomsky 1994:

(5)
Move raises α to a position β only if morphological properties of α itself
would not otherwise be satisfied in the derivation.

This definition raises a number of questions of interpretation, to which I will
return in chapter 5. Without going into the details for now, it is clear that this formulation of Greed is global. In order to know whether to apply Move to a constituent α, it is necessary to know whether the features of α would be satisfied
in an alternative derivation in which Move α did not apply. In chapter 5, I will
show that it is possible to redefine Greed in a local way while maintaining its
empirical effects.

Now consider the condition Procrastinate, which favors covert movement
over overt movement. Chomsky (1993: 30; 1994: 428) makes the assumption
that Procrastinate selects among convergent derivations. Overt movement can
occur, if otherwise the derivation would not converge. Limiting Procrastinate
to operate within the set of convergent derivations renders the condition global.
In order to decide whether to apply Move (at a particular stage in the derivation Σ), it is necessary to consider a derivation where Move does not apply and
then to see whether this derivation crashes at PF. In other words, the application of Move depends on information that is available only at PF, and not at Σ.
I will offer an alternative analysis of the effects of Procrastinate in chapter 6.

Now consider Relativized Minimality (Rizzi 1990) or the Minimal Link
Condition (Chomsky 1994; Chomsky and Lasnik 1993). In the last of these papers, Chomsky and Lasnik simplify Rizzi's (1990) approach, reducing it to the
statement "Minimize chain links." If an otherwise legitimate target of movement is already occupied, the Minimal Link Condition (MLC) is violated. This
condition is clearly local. Deciding whether Move applies to a representation
depends only on the information available in that representation, as illustrated
in (6).

(6)

*John$_i$ is likely that it was told t$_i$ that Mary left.

"It is likely that John was told that Mary left."

According to the MLC in either Chomsky and Lasnik 1993 or Chomsky 1994, the sentence in (6) is unacceptable, since there is a closer landing site (the position occupied by *it*). Although this formulation of the MLC raises some difficult questions, it is clear that the MLC is a local economy condition. Deciding whether to apply Move to Σ depends only on the information available in Σ. That information consists of a list of where the potential landing sites are.

　　Now consider Kitahara's (1995) analysis of the strict cycle. Kitahara bases his analysis on the Shortest Derivation Requirement, given above as (4) and repeated here as (7).[12]

(7)　*Shortest Derivation Requirement*

Minimize the number of operations necessary for convergence.

Kitahara deduces the effects of the strict cycle from this condition, and from the definition of the operation Target:

(8)　*Target* α *(targeting a category* α*)*

a. Build a new phrase structure γ immediately dominating α.

b. Substitute a category β for a newly created empty Δ external to α.

This definition is meant to subsume all structure-building operations, both unary and binary generalized transformations, and the projection of non-branching structure.

　　Consider, from this perspective, the case of subject islands illustrated in (9).

(9)

*who$_2$ did you say that [pictures of t$_2$]$_1$ were stolen t$_1$

　　Assuming that extraction out of subjects is not permissible, we must prevent the derivation where extraction of *who* from the NP [pictures of who] precedes passivization.[13] This derivation (simplified somewhat) is illustrated in (10).

(10)

a. you said that [$_{Agr_SP}$ were stole [$_{NP}$ pictures of who]]

b. who$_2$ you said that [$_{Agr_SP}$ were stolen [$_{NP}$ pictures of t$_2$]]

c. who$_2$ you said that [$_{Agr_SP}$ [$_{NP}$ pictures of t$_2$]$_1$ were stolen t$_1$]

Here there has been no extraction from the subject. Traditionally, this derivation has been held to violate the strict cycle, since the movement of the NP in (10c) is countercyclic. This derivation should be compared to the cyclic derivation, illustrated in (11), where passive precedes *wh*-movement.

(11)

a. you said that [$_{Agr_sP}$ were stolen [$_{NP}$ pictures of who]]

b. you said that [$_{Agr_sP}$ [pictures of who$_2$]$_1$ were stolen t$_1$]

c. who$_2$ you said that [$_{Agr_sP}$ [$_{NP}$ pictures of t$_2$]$_1$ were stolen t$_1$]

Although this derivation obeys the strict cycle, it involves movement of the *wh*-phrase from the subject. In Kitahara's theory, the countercyclic operation involves more applications of Target α than the cyclic operation. The reason for this is, briefly, as follows: The countercyclic derivation in (10) involves an extra operation of Target α. In the countercyclic operation, the projection of the embedded Agr$_s$P and the raising of the NP [pictures of t$_2$] to Spec Agr$_s$P involve two different applications of Target α. In the cyclic derivation (11), both the projection of the embedded Agr$_s$P and the raising of the NP [pictures of who$_2$] are accomplished with one application of Target α.[14]

It is clear that the SDR is highly global. Counting the number of operations in two derivations and comparing them assumes that the whole derivation has been accomplished. Therefore, any decision about whether an operation OP may apply to a set of syntactic objects Σ (as part of an optimal derivation) is not based on information available in Σ.

Given these considerations, I cannot accept Kitahara's analysis of the strict cycle (because it relies on an economy condition that is not local). However, I agree with Kitahara that the strict cycle as a principle should be eliminated. Similarly, the extension condition of Chomsky 1993 should be eliminated. In chapter 5, I will propose a new way to deal with the strict cycle that follows from independently motivated constraints on phrase structure (the LCA of Kayne 1994).

Chomsky (1994) proposes a different yet still global analysis of the sentence in (9).[15] Chomsky compares the cyclic and the countercyclic derivations and notes that in both derivations the DP undergoes the same movement (A-movement to Spec Agr$_s$P). In the countercyclic derivation the movement of the *wh*-phrase *who* is longer in the sense that movement of the *wh*-phrase crosses more maximal projections than in the cyclic derivation. The problematic aspect of this account, as with Kitahara's account, is that it is very global. In particular, in order to decide whether to move the *wh*-phrase *who* in (10b) we must know whether there is some other derivation in which the movement of the *wh*-phrase would be shorter. Therefore, we must reject this solution.[16]

Chomsky (1995: 227) gives a definition of economy that is intermediate between global and local. A particular stage in the derivation is defined by Σ (the set of syntactic objects formed) and by N (the remaining part of the Numeration). In order to decide whether an operation OP may apply to Σ and N (as part of an optimal derivation), we consider the set derivations that are continuations of the derivation that resulted in Σ and N. If OP is part of the most optimal derivation included in this set, the OP may apply. Clearly this definition is global according to the definition in (3), since deciding whether OP is in the optimal derivation involves looking at other derivations. However, it is not as global as the economy condition in (4), since it restricts the set of compared derivations to the continuations of a particular stage in the derivation.

In the course of this book, we will see many other global economy constraints that have been proposed. In each case, an alternative analysis that does not rely on global economy will be given.[17]

1.3   An Overview of Local Economy

The final result of this book will be that there are only two real economy conditions, both of which are local:

(12)   *Last Resort*
An operation OP involving α may apply only if some property of α is satisfied.

(13)   *Minimality*
An operation OP (satisfying Last Resort) may apply only if there is no smaller operation OP' (satisfying Last Resort).

Most other conceivable economy conditions are global and are therefore ruled out.

I will essentially follow three different strategies for eliminating global economy. First, I will show how the phenomena explained in terms of global economy can be more naturally explained in terms of independently motivated conditions. For example, chapter 4 shows how the effects of the strict cycle follow from Kayne's (1994) LCA. Second, I will show how some global economy conditions—for example, Chomsky's (1994) Greed—may be restated in local terms. Third, I will show how some global economy conditions may be completely replaced by local conditions of a quite different character. For example, in chapter 6, I suggest that the effects of Procrastinate in expletive constructions follow from a principle of chain formation (a principle that is itself one of a set of chain-formation principles).

I speculate that (12) and (13) above are the only real economy conditions, therefore giving economy a limited but important role in grammatical theory. In this book I will address many questions about these two conditions. For example, is there any interaction between them? I assume that there is no interaction, in the sense that every operation must meet both of the conditions. In this sense the economy conditions are independent. However, there is a natural hierarchy that can be imposed on the conditions: Last Resort determines when an operation is possible. If the operation is possible, Minimality determines the smallest one. Therefore, Minimality could be restated as a requirement that operations satisfying Last Resort be minimal.

I will also assume in this book that (12) and (13) are inviolable—in other words, that they can never be overridden. To clarify, consider the assumption (Chomsky 1994: 428) that Procrastinate selects among convergent derivations. We could make the same assumption about Minimality and Last Resort. In other words, we could rephrase Minimality as in (14).

(14) *Minimality*
An operation OP in derivation D may apply only if there no smaller operation OP′ in D′, and both D and D′ converge.

Clearly this is unacceptable from the standpoint of local economy. It would mean that, in order to decide whether an operation OP (applying to Σ) is part of the optimal derivation, we would have to know whether OP is part of a convergent derivation. To know this, we would have to look at the PF and LF representations of the derivation.

It may be asked whether local economy throws any light on the question of optionality. To a certain extent it does. As I will show in chapters 2 and 3, apparent cases of optional inversion are allowed by local economy and disallowed by global economy. As a general assessment, global economy tends to eliminate most cases of optionality, since an optional movement always results in a longer derivation.[18] From a local perspective, the only thing that matters is that each step satisfies the local economy conditions of Minimality and Last Resort (and perhaps others). To the extent that local economy is satisfied, optional movements are allowed.[19]

1.4 Outline

In chapters 2 and 3, I will show that inversion phenomena of several types constitute definite empirical consequences which follow from adopting a local as opposed to a global definition of economy. In particular, I will discuss locative inversion and quotative inversion. These are illustrated in (15) and (16).

(15)
a.   John rolled down the hill.
b.   Down the hill rolled John.

(16)
a.   "I am so happy," Mary thought.
b.   "I am so happy," thought Mary.

It is possible to show that the inverted derivation in (15b) and (16b) involves one more step than the non-inverted derivation in (15a) and (16a). Therefore, global economy (in particular, the Shortest Derivation Requirement) would block inversion in these cases.

In chapter 4, I will show how local economy can be extended in a natural way to Merge (as well as to Move). For example, I will show how binary branching can be viewed as the consequence of Minimality's applying to Merge. In addition, I will show that there is no need for a global economy account of the strict cycle (*contra* Chomsky 1994 and Kitahara 1995). Rather, the strict cycle may be deduced from independently needed conditions on phrase structure.

In chapter 5, I will show how local economy forces us to rethink the Last Resort condition and the analysis of successive cyclic movement. The resulting analysis of successive cyclic movement forces me to define feature checking as potentially asymmetric. I will show in this chapter that the ban on improper movement can be derived in part from Last Resort.

In chapter 6, I will consider the evidence for Procrastinate, which is inherently global (as discussed in section 1.2). I will discuss alternative local ways of analyzing the data that Procrastinate has been used to account for.

Chapter 2

Assumptions

In this chapter I will set out the assumptions needed to analyze locative inversion and quotative inversion. I will show that, on these assumptions, global economy predicts that locative inversion and quotative inversion should not be allowed. Locative inversion is discussed at the end of this chapter; quotative inversion will be discussed in chapter 3.

In section 2.1, I discuss the Extended Projection Principle, and show how a number of studies converge on how it is to be characterized. In section 2.2, I give my assumptions about clause structure. Basically, I follow Chomsky (1995) and Ura (1996) in assuming a clause structure based on multiple specifiers rather than on Agr projections. In sections 2.3–2.5, I introduce the basic economy conditions Last Resort and Minimality and discuss their properties. In section 2.6, I show the relevance of locative inversion to global economy. This discussion will set the stage for the more extensive discussion of quotative inversion in chapter 3.

Many of the assumptions made in this chapter will be discussed in much more detail in chapters 4–6, where they will be motivated and generalized.

2.1 The Extended Projection Principle

One important assumption for the analysis of both locative inversion and quotative inversion is that the Case feature of T and the EPP (Extended Projection Principle) are unrelated in that they can be satisfied independently. This is not at all obvious, as can be seen from (1).

(1)
John rolled down the hill.

In this sentence, *John* checks the nominative Case of T and satisfies the EPP (the property that Spec T must be filled overtly). If this were the only sentence that we had, it would be impossible to justify divorcing these two properties. Fortunately, expletive constructions and locative inversion argue strongly that the EPP and nominative Case should be separated (also, Exceptional Case Marking and successive cyclic movement[1] give independent support for an independent EPP).

Consider first expletive constructions, such as (2).

(2)
There are people in the garden.

If *there* checked the nominative Case feature of T, then T would not have any Case feature to check against *people*. Since *people* has a Case feature (that needs to be checked), we conclude that *there* does not have a Case feature.[2] Similarly, *there* cannot check the ϕ-features of the auxiliary *is*, since there would be no ϕ-features to check against *people*, and agreement between the verb and the post-verbal DP would not be accounted for. One possible analysis consistent with these observations is that *there* satisfies the EPP feature of T. Chomsky (1995: 232) suggests that the EPP feature of T is a strong D feature that is checked off against a DP in its checking domain (see section 2.4 for more details). This entails that the ϕ-features of the auxiliary and the Case feature of T are weak, since there is no overt movement of the DP that checks these features.[3]

This analysis is consistent with Branigan's (1993) analysis of locative inversion. Consider (3).

(3)
Down the hill rolled John.

Branigan proposes to divorce the EPP from nominative Case checking. According to Branigan, the EPP feature (of Agr_C on Branigan's theory) is checked by the fronted PP. The Case feature of the post-verbal subject *John* is checked after *John* raises at LF (to Spec Agr_S on Branigan's theory). The raising of *John* at LF accounts for the fact that *John* has nominative Case (as can be seen in the slightly marginal "down the hill rolled HE") and for the fact that the verb agrees with *John*.[4] Therefore, locative inversion and expletive constructions present strong evidence that the EPP and nominative Case should be divorced, contrary to what the simple sentence in (1) would lead us to believe. The EPP feature of T is strong and the Case feature of T is weak in English. One speculation is that the Case features of T are weak universally. Since this is the strongest assumption, I will adopt it.

2.2   Clause Structure

I will assume that the structure of the clause is basically as shown in (4).[5]

(4)

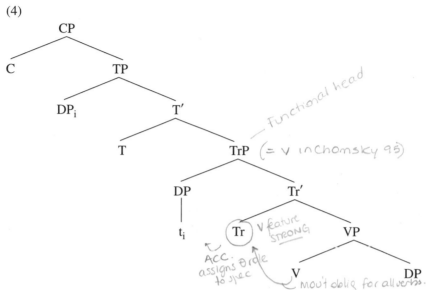

This structure assumes that the external argument is not generated under the VP with the direct object but, rather, is generated as the specifier of a head that I will call Tr (transitivity). This head is a generalization of the CAUS head proposed by Collins and Thráinsson (1993, 1995) for the analysis of double object constructions. It is the same head identified as v (light verb) by Chomsky (1995, chapter 4) and as Voi by Kratzer (1994).[6] I make following assumptions about this head: For transitive verbs, it checks accusative Case and assigns the external θ-role to its specifier. For unaccusative verbs, it is present, but it checks no accusative Case and assigns no external θ-role.[7] For all verbs, movement of V to adjoin to Tr is obligatory; therefore the V feature of Tr is strong (perhaps universally).

It seems natural to regard Tr as a functional head. Below, I assume that object shift is triggered by a strong D feature of Tr. Since parametric variation of feature values is usually restricted to functional heads, it follows that Tr is functional.

It may seem counterintuitive to postulate that an unaccusative verb phrase is the complement of Tr. There is straightforward empirical evidence that this is so. Consider (5), which involves an expletive construction with an unaccusative verb.

(5)
There arrived a man to the party.

In this sentence the unaccusative verb *arrive* precedes the post-verbal DP. Now consider the assumption (basically following Hale and Keyser 1993) that the theme should occupy the Spec VP position, and the locative the complement position of VP. These assumptions determine the following structure for the VP:

(6)

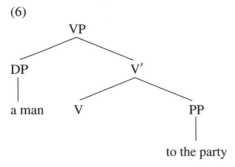

Given this structure, the natural prediction would be that the word order of an expletive construction should be "there a man arrived to the party." Since this is not the correct word order, I postulate that, even in the case of unaccusatives, there is a higher Tr head, to which the verb moves. This gives for (5) the structure shown in (7).

(7)

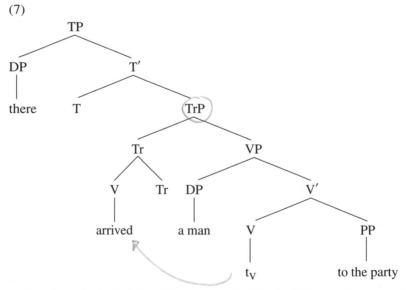

One important point about the structure in (4) is that it has no Agr projections. The most straightforward evidence for the Agr projections has always been that they provide landing sites for object shift. Consider in this connection the examples of object shift in Icelandic given in (8).

(8)

a. Jón   las   bækurnar   ekki.   *overt object shift.*
John   read   the books   not
"John did not read the books."

b. Jón   las   ekki   bækurnar.
John   read   not   the books
"John did not read the books."

In (8a), the object has shifted over negation. In (8b), the object has remained *in situ*. I return to the optionality of object shift in chapter 6. Here, let us assume that negation is adjoined to Tr′. I follow Chomsky (1995, chapter 4) in assuming that object shift moves the direct object to an outer specifier position of Tr. Note that we are assuming—following Chomsky (1994, 1995) and Ura (1994, 1996)—that each head may, in principle, have several specifier positions.

Recall that in section 2.1, following Chomsky (1995) and Branigan (1993), I proposed that nominative Case is (perhaps universally) weak, and that overt subject raising is motivated by an strong EPP feature of T. Similarly, in a language with overt object shift, the parallel assumption would be to assume that Tr must have a strong D feature to force the overt raising, and that the accusative Case feature of Tr is weak.[8] This assumption will provide the basis for my discussion of quotative inversion in English. Under these assumptions, the structure of the overt object shift sentence in (8a) (omitting possible movement to Spec CP, and all head movement) is as shown in (9).

(9)

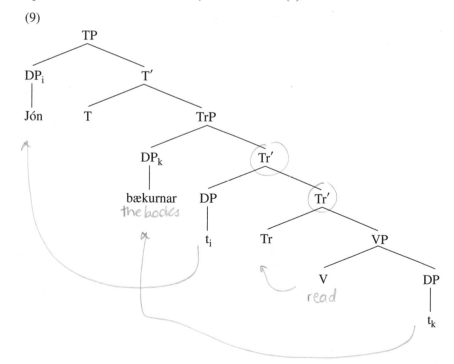

This structure for object shift bears more of a resemblance to the proposals of Holmberg (1986: 219) than to the proposals assuming that object shift moves a direct object into Spec Agr_O.[9] Holmberg proposed that object shift in Icelandic adjoins the shifted object to the VP.

I believe it is possible to state the analyses of this book in either the Spec Agr_O theory or the multiple-specifier theory. The multiple-specifier theory tends to simplify representations and derivations. In addition Chomsky (1995) presents some conceptual arguments for a multiple-specifier theory (which I will not recapitulate here). However, at various points in the book I will use clause structure based on Agr_O in discussing particular structures and examples for the sake of ease of presentation.

The Agr_O theory and the multiple-specifier theory have many aspects in common. First, both involve multiple specifier positions. In the Agr theory, the two positions are Spec Agr_O and Spec VP. In the other theory, the Tr head has two specifier positions. Second, on both theories the checking of accusative Case takes place in a specifier position that is above the θ-position of the subject. Third, both analyses rely on a notion of equidistance (discussed below) to make sure that the direct object may shift to its Case position. In the Agr_O theory, the notion of equidistance involves head chains. In the multiple-specifier theory, the notion of equidistance involves two specifiers of the same head being equidistant. Given these similarities, it will not be surprising to find that analyses in one framework may be translated into analyses in the other. I discuss more points of comparison below.[10]

One difference between the two approaches is that Chomsky's (1993) analysis of the relation between verb movement (to Agr_O and T), and object shift is lost. Chomsky proposed that if the verb moves to Agr_O, the derived chain (V, t_V) renders Spec Agr_O and Spec VP equidistant, thereby allowing the object to shift. However, since the two specifier positions of Tr are in the minimal domain of Tr they are always equidistant (this is described in more detail in section 2.4). Since object shift in Icelandic is not the primary phenomenon that I wish to explain in this book, this particular shortcoming of the multiple-specifier approach will have little effect on the analyses presented here.

It has often been proposed that the position of the shifted object is below the θ-position of the subject (Travis 1992; Koizumi 1993). While this view is attractive in several respects, it is also untenable. Consider the sentences from Icelandic (Jonas and Bobaljik 1993: 93) shown in (10)–(12).

(10)

það	stingur	smjörinu	einhver	í vasann
There	put	the.butter	someone	in the.pocket

"Somebody put the butter in the pocket."

(11)

það	sagði	Sveini	einhver	sögu
there	told	Sveinn	somebody	a.story

"Somebody told Sveinn a story."

(12)

*það	sagði	Sveini	stúdent	sögu
There	told	Sveinn	a.student	a.story

"Somebody told Sveinn a story."

As (10) and (11) show, apparently the subject DP *einhver* "somebody" (and perhaps a few others, e.g., *allir* "everyone" and *enginn* "nobody") may appear after the shifted object in an object shift construction. This construction has not been extensively investigated, and it is not clear what class of subjects show the same behavior. In spite of this, the construction provides straightforward evidence for the position of the shifted object with respect to the *in situ* position of the subject. The fact that the subject does not appear at the end of the sentence indicates that it has not been extraposed. The simplest explanation for this data is that in (10) and (11) the subject remains *in situ* while the object shifts either to Spec Agr_O or to the outer specifier of Tr.

2.3 Last Resort

As was mentioned in chapter 1, local economy is reduced to two general conditions on all operations (Merge or Move): Minimality and Last Resort. I will assume the definition of Last Resort given in (13).

(13)
Move raises α to the checking domain of a head H with a feature F only if the feature F of H enters into a checking relation with a feature F of α.

This definition is basically from Collins 1995. (For much additional discussion, see chapter 4 of Chomsky 1995 and Lasnik 1995.) I will provide more motivation for this condition in chapter 4, where I will generalize it to cases of pure Merge. In chapter 5, I will show that ECM and successive cyclic movement provide evidence for this condition. The intuition behind this definition is that a constituent is moved only if its movement will result in some syntactic work being done.

This definition of Last Resort presupposes a definition of checking domain and checking relation. The definition of checking domain—which will not be modified in this book—is given in (14).

Chapter 2

(14)

Let H be a functional head dominating a feature F. The checking domain of F consists of

a. X adjoined to H and any features dominated by X

b. any XP in Spec H, and any features dominated by X.

(See Chomsky 1995: 255, 268.)

The definition of checking relation is given in (15).

(15)

F1 and F2 enter a checking relation iff F2 is in the checking domain of F1 and F1 is deleted. (F2 may also be deleted.)

The presupposition of this definition is that deletion is always under identity, so that F1 will delete only if identical to F2. Note that there is no operation of *checking* in these definitions. Rather, there are a notion of deletion, a notion of checking relation (where at least one of the features deletes), and a notion of checking domain (where checking relations are established). It would be more accurate to use the phrases "deletion relation" and "deletion domain." However, given the established usage, I will stick to the phrases "checking relation" and "checking domain," and I will sometimes use the expression "F1 checks F2" to mean that F1 and F2 have entered into a checking relation and F2 deletes.

In the case where only F1 (not F2) is deleted, I will say that we have an asymmetric checking relation. The concept of asymmetric checking is the foundation for successive cyclic movement, ECM, and multiple feature checking, as will be discussed in more detail in chapter 5. Deletion of F means that the feature F is invisible to any operations at the interfaces (LF and PF) and to any other operations.[11]

2.3.1 Interpretable Features

The above definitions of Last Resort and checking relation incorporate the notion of asymmetric feature checking. This means that it is possible that two features F1 and F2 enter into a checking relation and that only one of these features actually deletes. This basic notion of asymmetric feature checking is due to Collins (1994, 1995). However, Chomsky (1995) presents a much more articulated theory of features that puts asymmetric feature checking on firm ground. Since I will be discussing this theory in much greater detail in chapter 5, I will only give a brief presentation here in order to provide the necessary assumptions for the analysis of locative inversion and quotative inversion.

The features that enter into interpretation at LF are interpretable, while the others are uninterpretable[12] and must be eliminated for convergence. Using this characterization of interpretable features, Chomsky gives the following categorization. The interpretable features are categorial features (+/–V, +/–N, D, T, etc.), the φ-features of N (person, number, gender) and the [+*wh*] feature of a *wh*-phrase. Each of these features plays some role in interpretation. The uninterpretable features are the Case features of a N, the φ-features and Case features of V and T, any strong feature, and any other feature not listed under the set of interpretable features.

Since interpretable features are needed at LF, they cannot be deleted. On the other hand, uninterpretable features must be deleted. Given these assumptions (which will be more fully discussed in chapter 5), consider (16) and (17).

(16)
John rolled down the hill.

(17)
There are people in the garden.

In (16), *John* moves to Spec T. This movement satisfies Last Resort, since the strong EPP feature of T enters into a checking relation with the D feature of DP. The strong EPP feature (being uninterpretable) is deleted in this checking relation. The D feature of DP (being interpretable) is not deleted. This is a case of asymmetric feature checking. Simultaneously, the Case feature of *John* enters into a checking relation with the Case-assigning feature of T. Although the Case-assigning feature of T is weak, we may assume that once a feature F1 occupies the checking domain of a feature F2, then F1 and F2 may enter into a checking relation if F1 and F2 are identical.[13] Since both features are uninterpretable, they both delete. This is a case of symmetric feature checking.

At LF, the verb raises to T, where its φ-features enter into a checking relation with the φ-features of the DP. Since the φ-features of the DP cannot delete (being interpretable), this is a case of asymmetric feature checking.

In (17), *there* is merged into Spec T. In this position, the D feature of *there* enters into a checking relation with the EPP feature of T. Since the EPP feature of T is uninterpretable, it is deleted. Whether the D feature of the expletive is deleted depends on whether this feature is interpretable. I will assume for the sake of uniformity with other DPs that the D feature of the expletive is not deleted.[14] This is then a case of asymmetric feature checking.

The Case feature of T and the φ-features of the auxiliary verb *are* have not yet been deleted. Still following Chomsky (1995, chapter 4), I assume that the formal features of the post-verbal DP *people* raise and adjoin to T at LF. These formal features—written FF(people)—consist of the Case feature, φ-features, and D feature of *people*. The resulting structure of T is shown in (18).

(18)

FF(DP)   T

In this configuration, the Case feature of the DP is in the checking domain of the Case feature of T, a checking relation is established and both features are deleted (being uninterpretable). This is a case of symmetric feature checking.

After the auxiliary (or simply its formal features) raises to T, the φ-features of DP will be in the checking domain of the agreement features of the auxiliary. The φ-features of the auxiliary will be deleted (being uninterpretable), while the φ-features of the DP will not be deleted. Thus, this is a case of asymmetric feature checking.

2.4 Minimality

The other basic local economy condition is Minimality, defined in (19).[15]

(19)
α can raise to a target K only if there is no operation (satisfying Last Resort) Move β targeting K, where β is closer to K.

This condition is basically taken from Ura (1995) and Chomsky (1995, chapter 4),[16] although I do not assume that it is built into the definition of Attract, as does Chomsky (1995: 297). I will return to this point in section 2.5.

Note that Minimality applies only if Last Resort has been met. This is a natural hierarchy of these conditions. It is possible to choose the minimal operation only if it is known that each relevant operation is motivated. Later on, when verifying whether a particular operation satisfies Minimality, I will always make sure to show that Last Resort is satisfied too.

There is a certain asymmetry in this definition, in that a closer β blocks movement of α, but this definition seems to allow movement of α over heads that contain features that could check α. Collins and Branigan (1995) propose that such movement is not allowed. They state that movement of a constituent α over a head β is impossible if β has a feature that can enter into a checking relation with α. I will refer to this as symmetric Minimality. As will be seen, little in this book rests on which formulation of Minimality is adopted.

This definition presupposes a definition of *closer*, which I take from Chomsky (1995: 356) and Ura (1995)[17]:

(20)

If β c-commands α, and τ is the target of movement, then β is closer to τ than α unless β is in the same minimal domain as (i) τ or (ii) α.

The "unless" clauses in this definition define the notion of equidistance.[18] To see how this definition works intuitively, consider (21).

(21)

Move copies α and merges α as the sister of the target position τ. The intervening constituent β will not block the movement of α under one of two cases. If α and β are in the same minimal domain of some head, then movement of α will not be blocked. If τ and β are in the same minimal domain of some head, then movement of α will not be blocked either.

In the context of the Bantu Inversion construction, Ura 1996 gives extensive empirical support to these notions of Minimality and equidistance.[19]

Consider how the definition in (20) works in the context of overt object shift. The structure illustrated in (22) is an intermediate structure leading to (9).

(22)

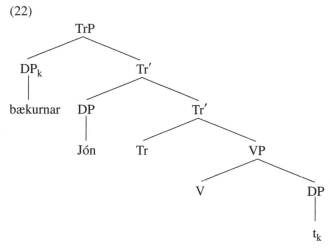

Here the DP *bækurnar* "the books" (which is the complement of V) moves into the outside specifier of Tr, where its accusative Case feature and its D feature enter into checking relations with the Case feature and the strong D feature of Tr, thereby satisfying Last Resort.

This movement satisfies Minimality, since the subject in the inner specifier of Tr and the outer specifier of Tr are in the minimal domain of Tr. Therefore, the *in situ* subject (which has an undeleted D feature) does not block object shift (although the subject could, in principle, have raised to check the D feature of Tr).

Now consider the movement of the subject to Spec T. This movement results in the structure illustrated in (9), which is repeated here as (23).

(23)

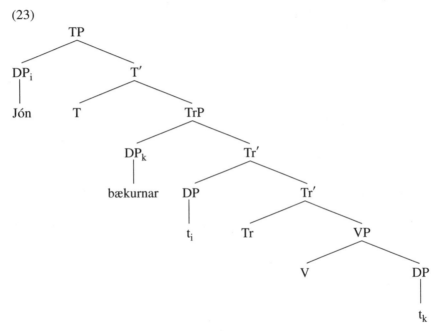

This movement satisfies Minimality: Since the DP *bækurnar* "the books" and the subject (before movement) are both in the minimal domain of Tr, the DP *bækurnar* "the books" does not count as a closer DP to Spec T (although the shifted object has an undeleted D feature that could, in principle, raise to Spec T to enter into a checking relation with the EPP feature of T).

There is no trivial way to state the dependence of object shift on verb movement that is found in Icelandic in this system (see Chomsky 1993). Nor is there any way to state the dependence of object shift on an available Spec TP position (as found in Jonas and Bobaljik 1993). However, other generalizations are expressible. For example, crossing path movement (where the underlying subject moves to the outer specifier of Tr and the underlying object moves to Spec T) is still not allowed. (See Chomsky 1995: 357 for more discussion.)

2.5   Attract versus Move

Chomsky (1995) postulates that Last Resort and Minimality are part of the definition of the operation he calls Attract (which is meant to supplant Move). This definition is given in (24).

(24)
K attracts F if F is the closest feature that can enter into a checking relation with a sublabel of K.

Before addressing Chomsky's reasons for incorporating Last Resort and Minimality into the definition of Attract (replacing movement), I will give a number reasons why such a definition is not desirable.

First, in the system I am developing, there are very simple operations, such as Merge, Copy (which is always a reflex of Merge), and Delete. The complicated facts concerning movement are the results of these very simple operations interacting with general principles, such as Last Resort and Minimality. Under this way of looking at things, we may expect the general principles to apply not only to movement but also to cases of pure Merge. This is in fact the claim of chapter 4, where it is argued that pure Merge satisfies Last Resort and Minimality. If Last Resort and Minimality were parts of the definition of Attract (supplanting Move), then they would independently have to be part of the definition of pure Merge. Such a result would be odd. Both Attract and Merge would have exactly the same conditions built into them.

Second, we may expect conditions like Last Resort and Minimality to operate in morphology (governing the placement of second-position clitics and the rearrangement of affixes) and phonology (governing deletion and epenthesis and the placement of prosodically determined affixes). This would be the optimal result: very general conditions, restricting all linguistic systems. However, if Last Resort and Minimality were part of the definition of Attract, we would not necessarily expect to see these conditions operate outside the domain of syntactic movement.

Now let us consider Chomsky's reasons for defining Attract as incorporating Last Resort and Minimality. First, Chomsky (1995: 296) says that the Minimal Link Condition (our Minimality) has the property that it is inviolable. In other words, it does not choose the optimal derivation from among just the convergent derivations. This means that we do not expect a situation where a violation of the MLC is allowed, if otherwise the derivation would crash. If the MLC was part of the definition of Attract/Move, this property would be explained. Every operation would obey the MLC as a matter of definition. However, on the theory of economy that I am developing here, no economy condition selects the optimal derivation from among convergent derivations (this type of selection being a global notion).

Chomsky (1995: 268) raises the question of how two derivations could be compared if they had shorter links in different places. (See example (9) and derivations (10) and (11) in chapter 1 above.) If MLC was part of the definition of Attract/Move, no such comparison would ever be possible. Similarly, under the definition of local economy, if Minimality is a local economy condition, it could never compare operations that apply in two different derivations at all.

Chomsky (1995: 253) lists several properties that he assumes are part of the definition of Move. These include c-command, uniformity and Last Resort. According to Chomsky, these conditions will never be overridden for convergence, since they are not economy conditions, rather they are part of the definition of Move. As far as Last Resort is concerned, in the system of this book, no economy condition may be overridden for the sake of convergence, since that is a global notion. Thus, there is no difficulty in maintaining Last Resort as an economy condition from this point of view.

Now consider c-command. It seems to be the case that a moved α always c-commands its trace. This generalization has variously been called the Proper Binding Condition, or has been incorporated into the Empty Category Principle. One way to account for this fact is to assume that c-command is part of the definition of Move. However, this would clearly be missing the generalization that most cases of downward and sideways movement are ruled out by completely independent conditions. For example, overt downward movement would violate the strict cycle (which reduces to the LCA, on the theory presented in chapter 4). A quantifier-like expression (such as *which man*) always moves to a c-commanding position, presumably for reasons of interpretation. The only remaining cases are covert downward head movement and covert downward A-movement. However, it is extremely difficult to find genuine examples of this kind of movement that are not ruled out by completely independent conditions. Therefore, I assume that c-command is not part of the definition of Move.[20]

Therefore, it is reasonable to maintain the simplest definition of Move (Copy + Merge) and to derive the properties of Move (such as c-command, Last Resort and Minimality) from general principles.

2.6 Locative Inversion

In this section, I will give a formal account of locative inversion based on the background assumptions presented above. This account will pave the way for my analysis of quotative inversion, which has much in common with locative inversion. Consider the sentences in (25). which involve locative inversion.[21]

(25)
a.   Down the hill rolled John.
b.   John rolled down the hill.

The fundamental dilemma posed by this pair of sentences is that both of the word orders seemed be allowed. In a derivational theory where derivations are constrained by global economy (such as the Shortest Derivation Requirement of chapter 1), the question is whether the inverted (25a) and the non-inverted (25b) sentence have derivations of the same length.[22]

In order to analyze locative inversion, I will need a few assumptions. First, I assume (controversially) that locative inversion is restricted to unaccusative verbs.[23] This will simplify the following account a great deal. Given this assumption, consider (25a). At the point in the derivation after the construction of TrP and the operation Merge(T, TrP), we will have the structure shown in (26).

(26)

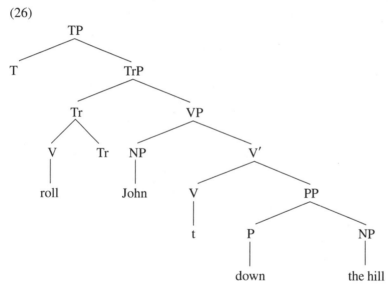

As was outlined above, movement of *John* to Spec T satisfies Last Resort. Now consider the derivation of the locative inversion sentence in (25a). In this derivation the PP must move to Spec T. We must verify that this movement satisfies Last Resort and Minimality. Assuming for the moment that Last Resort is satisfied, consider Minimality. As Ura (1996) points out, both *John* in Spec VP and the PP are in the minimal domain of the same head (the verb). From this and from the definition of Minimality in (19) and (20) above, it follows that *John* does not block movement of the PP to Spec T, even though *John* has a D feature that could enter into a checking relation with the strong EPP feature of T.[24]

Now consider Last Resort. We must show that the PP enters into a checking relation with the EPP feature of T in some way. This is what allows movement of the PP from its VP-internal position to Spec T to satisfy Last Resort. This analysis seems to run counter to Chomsky's (1995: 232) assumption that it is the D feature of a DP that enters into a checking relation with the EPP feature of T.

I can see two ways to allow the PP to enter into a checking relation with T.

First, consider the possibility that it is the DP *the hill,* which is complement of the PP, that is entering into a checking relation with the EPP feature of T in (25a). This would entirely analogous to the fact that *wh*-movement in question formation can pied-pipe a PP, as shown in (27).

(27)
Under which bed did Betty hide the candy?

In this expression, the [+*wh*] feature of the *wh*-phrase enters into a checking relation with the strong Q feature. The strong Q feature deletes (strength being uninterpretable), and the [+*wh*] feature remains (being interpretable). What is odd is that a checking relation is established, in spite of the fact that it is a PP that is in Spec CP, and not the *wh*-phrase itself. Apparently, a feature of the complement of a PP may enter into a checking relation external to the PP.

Applying this generalization to locative inversion (whatever its ultimate explanation), we could say that in (25a) the PP is pied-piped to Spec T, and that the EPP feature of T enters a checking relation with the D feature of *the hill*, which is the complement of the PP. The movement of the PP would thereby satisfy Last Resort. This analysis leaves us with the question of why the verb in (25a) does not agree with the complement of the PP (as shown by the unacceptability of "down the hills roll John"). One solution is to simply stipulate that nominative Case is always assigned under agreement. This can be formalized in the following way: The Case-assigning feature of T may enter into a checking relation with the Case feature of some DP only if either the ϕ-features of T or the ϕ-features of a V adjoined to T enters into a checking relation with the ϕ-features of DP. I will simply leave this as an option, without developing it at this point.

A second possibility is to allow the set of features that may enter into a checking relation with the EPP feature of T to be widened from simply the D feature of a DP to any categorial feature. Under this analysis, the movement of the PP would satisfy Last Resort, since the P feature of the PP would enter into a checking relation with the EPP feature of T, which would delete.[25]

Let us then assume that the movement of the PP to Spec T satisfies Last Resort and Minimality. This movement yields the representation shown in (28).

(28)

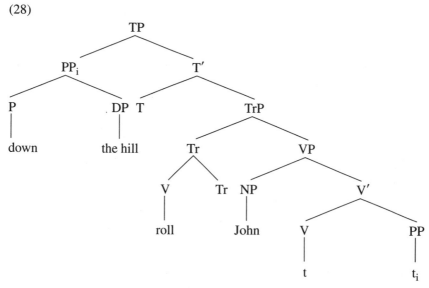

Note that this structure automatically gives us an explanation of the PP V DP word order of locative inversion. The DP follows the verb, since the verb raises and adjoins to Tr overtly.

There are still some uninterpretable features that have not been deleted: the Case feature of the subject, the Case-assigning feature of T (which is weak), and the φ-features of the verb.

At LF, the formal features of *John* (including the Case feature, the φ-features, and the D feature) raise and adjoin to T. The Tr has also raised and adjoined to T. Therefore, the Case feature of *John* is in the checking domain of the Case-assigning feature of T. A checking relation is established, and both features are deleted. The φ-features of the verb enter a checking relation with the φ-features of *John*, which are part of FF(John)), and are deleted. Therefore, no uninterpretable features remain, and the derivation converges.[26]

2.6.1 Locative Inversion and Global Economy
I will now compare the inverted and non-inverted derivations in summary form. First, the non-inverted derivation has the steps shown in (29).

(29)
a. V raises and adjoins to Tr
b. DP raises to Spec T
c. Tr raises and adjoins to T covertly

This derivation has three movement operations. (I leave out the instances of pure Merge, since they are common to both the inverted and non-inverted derivation.) It is important to note that movement of DP to Spec T (a single movement operation) results in deletion of both the Case feature and the EPP feature of T.

Now consider the steps in the inverted derivation:

(30)
a. V raises and adjoins to Tr
b. PP raises to Spec TP
c. Tr raises and adjoins to T covertly
d. FF(John) raise and adjoin to T covertly

This derivation has four movement operations. It is important to note that the Case feature and the EPP feature of T are deleted by virtue of two different movement operations. This is the reason that the inverted derivation has four steps: movement of the PP to Spec T is an inherently wasteful operation, since it does not result in simultaneous deletion of the Case feature and the EPP feature of T.

It is easily seen that the derivation of the inverted word order is longer than the derivation of the non-inverted word order. Suppose that we were to adopt the assumption (Chomsky 1995: 227) that the reference set for determining the optimal derivation is determined by the Numeration. Clearly, the inverted and non-inverted derivations are based on the same lexical choices.[27] If we were to adopt the Shortest Derivation Requirement (chapter 1 above), the inverted derivation would be blocked. Therefore, we would predict that the inverted derivation would not be allowed, contrary to fact. Therefore, locative inversion provides good evidence against global economy.

Does local economy fare any better in accounting for the two word orders in (25)? I have already shown that it does. All the movements in both derivations satisfy Last Resort and Minimality, the only two local economy conditions I have so far postulated.

I conclude that, in the analysis of locative inversion, local economy is superior to global economy in its predictions. This model of reasoning is exactly what will be applied in the next chapter to the more complicated case of quotative inversion.

Chapter 3

Quotative Inversion

Quotative inversion, illustrated in (1), is used with verbs that have direct speech complements.

(1)
a. "I am so happy," Mary thought.
b. "I am so happy," thought Mary.

In (1b) the verb precedes the subject. I will argue that this results from an operator coindexed with the quote undergoing movement into Spec T, where it checks the EPP feature of T.

There appear to be two alternative derivations involving the same lexical items (the same Numeration): one in which inversion occurs (1a) and one in which it does not (1b). I will show that global economy predicts that the derivation with inversion should not occur. Since the derivation with inversion does occur, this counts as an argument against global economy.

Most of the data on quotative inversion in this chapter are from Collins and Branigan 1995, which is a development of Branigan and Collins 1993. Some of the empirical generalizations and a preliminary analysis in terms of verb movement to C appear in Collins 1992. I make four major departures from Collins and Branigan 1995: First, I assume that the quotative operator undergoes movement to Spec TP. Second, I give an entirely different account of the "transitivity restriction." Third, I show the relevance of local economy for the analysis of the construction. Fourth, I assume a clause structure based on multilple specifiers, not on Agr projections. (However, I believe that the analysis I give of quotative inversion could be restated fairly easily in an Agr-based theory.) Other departures from Collins and Branigan 1995 will be made clear throughout the chapter.

In section 3.1, I motivate the basic structural analysis of quotative inversion, giving tests that indicate the location of the subject, the verb and the quote. In section 3.2, I discuss the basic derivation of quotative inversion. In section 3.3,

I discuss the relevance of local economy for the analysis of quotative inversion. In section 3.4, I present an analysis of the transitivity constraint found in quotative inversion. Because the last section depends heavily on the analysis of double object constructions, I review and revise the analysis presented in Collins and Thráinsson 1993 and Collins and Thráinsson 1995.

3.1 Structure of Quotative Inversion

In this section, I will briefly present the evidence that motivates the positions of the various constituents in quotative inversion constructions. A more comprehensive discussion of the data may be found in Collins and Branigan 1995.

The three principal constituents whose positions must be investigated are the subject, the verb, and the quote. I will investigate each of these constituents in turn.

3.1.1 The Position of the Subject
The sentences in (2) and (3) show that if the verb has a PP complement the subject must precede these complements in quotative inversion.

(2)
a. "Where to?" asked the driver of the passenger.
b. *"Where to?" asked of the passenger the driver.

(3)
a. "John left," said the student to Mary.
b. *"John left," said to Mary the student.

This fact rules out an analysis of quotative inversion where the subject undergoes rightward extraposition from the Spec TP position to adjoin to TP (or VP). Under such an analysis, the sentences in (2b) and (3b) would be predicted to be acceptable. If the subject is long or heavy, then it may follow the complements of the verb. This is shown in (4).

(4)
a. "Where to?" asked of us the driver with the blond hair.
b. "John left," whispered to Joan the woman sitting at the end of the counter.

This fact recalls the basic facts concerning Heavy NP Shift. If a verb has both a DP complement and a PP complement, the DP may follow the PP if the DP is sufficiently long or heavy; this is illustrated in (5).

(5)

a. I put the box on the counter.

b. ??I put on the counter the box. (neutral intonation)

c. I put on the counter the box that Mary sent to me.

I suspect that any adequate analysis of HNPS will carry over to the sentences in (3) and (4), but this is a topic for later investigation.

In the framework that I am adopting, there are at least two positions to the left of the verbal complements that the subject may be occupying: Spec TrP and Spec TP. There is some evidence that the subject remains in the Spec TrP position, and does not raise to Spec TP. This evidence concerns the distribution of floated quantifiers. Consider the paradigm illustrated in (6) and (7).

(6)

a. "We must do this again," the guests all declared to Tony.

b. "We must do this again," declared all the guests to Tony.

c. *"We must do this again," declared the guests all to Tony.

(7)

a. "Do you have the time?," the bankers each asked.

b. "Do you have the time?" asked each of the bankers.

c. *"Do you have the time?" asked the bankers each.

Following Sportiche (1988), we may assume that the subject strands a quantifier as it undergoes A-movement to Spec TP. Therefore, in (6a) the floated quantifier has been stranded in Spec TrP after the DP has moved to Spec TP. The sentence (6b) shows that there is nothing problematic about a quantified DP appearing in a quotative inversion construction. The sentence (6c) shows that quotative inversion is unacceptable with a floated quantifier. One explanation of this fact is that in (6c), the subject remains in Spec TrP, so that a quantifier could not be stranded by A-movement. A similar paradigm is illustrated in (7).

Therefore, we can conclude that the subject in quotative inversion remains in Spec TrP. However, there is evidence that the subject moves out of Spec TrP at LF. Consider (8), which illustrates the Case and agreement properties of the subject in quotative inversion.

(8)

a. "Mary has already eaten," said ?he/?I/*me/*him.

b. "Mary has already left," says/*say John.

c. "Mary has already left," say/*says the two men.

Sentence (8a) shows that the post-verbal subject must have nominative Case. Sentences (8b) and (8c) show that the post-verbal subject must agree with the verb. In the framework that we are adopting, we conclude that the subject must be in the checking domain of T at LF. Below, I will argue that a quotative operator fills Spec T overtly and checks the EPP feature of T. Therefore, the only possibility is that the Case and ϕ-features of the subject raise and adjoin to T at LF (in other words, FF(Subj); see chapter 4 of Chomsky 1995).

Another argument that the subject remains in Spec TrP in quotative inversion is that the sentence in (8a) with nominative pronouns is not perfect. This may be attributed to a general cross-linguistic fact that pronouns tend to move overtly (Collins and Thráinsson 1993, 1995; Diesing 1995).

3.1.2   The Position of the Verb

There is straightforward evidence that the verb does not stay *in situ* (in VP or TrP) in quotative inversion. Consider again the following sentences:

(9)
a. "I am so happy," Mary thought.
b. "I am so happy," thought Mary.

If the subject is in Spec TrP (as shown in the preceding subsection), then the verb must have raised and adjoined to a position higher than TrP. This leaves C and T in our framework. I will assume that the verb moves no further than T.[1]

In generative grammar, the standard evidence for the position of a verb comes from considering its position with respect to negation and adverbs. Let us consider each of these factual domains in turn, beginning with the placement of negation in quotative inversion.

(10)
a. "Let's eat," said John just once.
b. "Let's eat," John said just once.
c. "Lets eat," John didn't say just once.
d. *"Let's eat," not said John just once.
e. *"Let's eat," said not John just once.
f. *"Let's eat," didn't John say just once. (See (24) below.)

Sentence (10c) illustrates the use of negation in a non-inverted quotative construction. This sentence is most acceptable when the negation is interpreted as negating the adverb (*not just once*). Sentences (10d)–(10f) show that quotative inversion is never possible if the sentence contains negation. Let us assume for negation the phrase structure illustrated in (11).

(11)

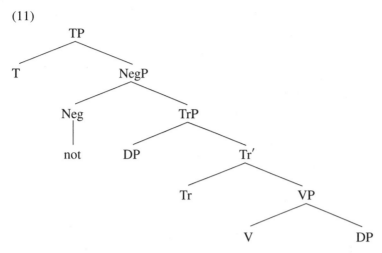

This structure immediately explains the unacceptability of (10d), since in (11) there is no position between Neg and the subject (in Spec Tr) for the verb to move to. The explanation of (10f) will be left until subsection 3.1.4.

Now consider (10e). In quotative inversion, the verb raises and adjoins to Tr, and then Tr raises and adjoins to T. Given that derivation, we can exclude (10e) using the Head Movement Constraint (Travis 1984, Chomsky 1986). Since the Neg head intervenes between Tr and T, no movement of Tr to T is possible.

There are two problems with this account. First, if we assume that the HMC reduces to Minimality (see chapter 2), then it is not clear how the Neg head blocks verb movement. Movement of the V to T satisfies the V feature of T. It is not clear what feature of T would be checked if Neg raised and adjoined to T. Therefore, movement of Neg to T would not satisfy Last Resort and could not block movement of V. Second, in the case of auxiliary verbs, verb movement over negation is allowed in English. This is illustrated by (12).

(12)
a. John is not a teacher.
b. John is not tall.

In these sentences, the auxiliary verb moves from the head of Tr to adjoin to T, raising over Neg (Pollock 1989; Chomsky 1991). If it is possible for an auxiliary to move over negation, then why isn't it possible for a main verb in (10e) to move over negation? Although I have no definitive account, I simply note that all accounts of the placement of negation in English have to make some stipulation concerning the difference between auxiliary verbs and main verbs. Consider, for example, (13).

(13)
*John not likes apples.

If we adopt the assumption that the verb *likes* moves to T at LF, then the unacceptability of (13) is accounted for if we assume that covert verb movement may not raise over negation. This is the strategy of Chomsky (1991). Alternatively, (13) may be blocked if we assume that a main verb may never raise over negation (whether or not the movement is overt). A reasonable speculation about the difference between the acceptable cases of verb movement in (12) and the unacceptable cases of verb movement in (13) is that (13) involves movement of a main verb rather than an auxiliary.

The account in Collins and Branigan 1995 is superior to my present account on this point. In Collins and Branigan 1995, the reason that (10e) is unacceptable is that the verb only raises to Agr_O in quotative inversion. If we assume that Neg is higher than Agr_O, (10e) follows immediately.

This point is related to a more general point comparing the multiple-specifier theory of clause structure and the Agr-projection theory of clause structure. In the Agr theory, there are two additional heads (Agr_S and Agr_O) that may be used as the landing sites of head movement. It might be expected that movement to these positions could be used in accounting for certain word-order facts (involving verb movement and clitic movement, for example). In fact, Pollock (1989) claimed that the fact that the distribution of negation differed from that of other adverbs in infinitives could be accounted for in terms of an Agr projection. In the multiple-specifier view of clause structure, we have lost this account. Similarly, the account of pronoun placement in particle constructions given in Collins and Thráinsson 1993 and in Collins and Thráinsson 1995 relied crucially on the presence of an Agr projection, in addition to the other functional projections.

Now consider the position of adverbs in quotative inversion structures, illustrated in (14) and (15).

(14)
a. "I finally quit this job," John murmured happily.
b.   murmured John happily.
c.   ?happily murmured John.
d.   *murmured happily John.

(15)
a. "I am leaving," John shouted abruptly.
b.   shouted John abruptly.
c.   ?abruptly shouted John.
d.   *shouted abruptly John.

The main generalization that emerges from these data is that the adverb may not appear between the verb and the subject in quotative inversion. The structure of (15d) would be as shown in (16).

(16)

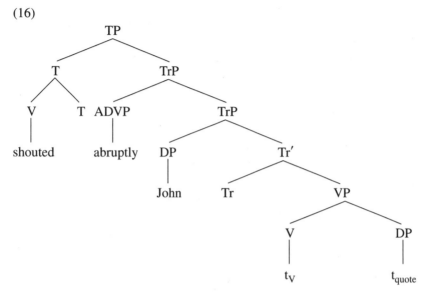

If we assume that an adverb may not be adjoined to TrP, these facts follow immediately. This assumption may be related to Chomsky's (1994) argument against adjunction to an XP that has a semantic role at LF. For example, adjunction to a DP argument will result in two DP segments, only one of which would be able to receive a semantic role at LF (the other being uninterpretable).[2]

The above analysis leaves open the position of the adverb in (14b) and (14c). One possibility is that the adverb in these sentences is adjoined to TP or to T', if these possibilities exist. In the case of the post-verbal adverb in (14b), it is also possible that the adverb occupies some kind of VP-internal position (as in Larson 1988). If we assume that the adverb in (14c) is adjoined to either TP or T', then that provides one argument that the verb has not moved to C in quotative inversion. If the verb moved to C, the order in (14c) would be unacceptable.

A potential problem with this analysis is illustrated by (17).

(17)
John will quickly leave the room.

Here an adverb appears between an auxiliary and the following verb. If the adverb in this sentence is adjoined to TrP, it counterexemplifies the claim made above that adverbs cannot adjoin to TrP. However, it would be equally plausible to claim that the adverb has adjoined to Tr' in (17), or that there is another functional projection of some type between the auxiliary *will* and the verb *leave* to which the adverb adjoins. I leave the decision between these possibilities for further research.

In this subsection I have given an analysis of the position of the verb in quotative inversion. I have tried to show that there is strong evidence that the verb raises out of TrP overtly (since it occurs to the left of the *in situ* subject). I have also given a preliminary analysis of the position of the verb with respect to negation and with respect to adverbs. The analysis of negation and adverbs in quotative inversion is made nontrivial by the minimal assumptions about clause structure that I adopt.

3.1.3 The Position of the Quote

There are at least the following three possibilities for the position of the quote in quotative inversion:

First, as was assumed in Collins and Branigan 1995, the quote could undergo direct movement to Spec CP. This assumption entails that Spec TP is not filled overtly—in other words, that T in quotative inversion does not have a strong EPP feature.

A second possibility is that the quote undergoes movement to Spec TP to check the strong EPP feature of T. This analysis is conceptually more desirable than the first in that it allows us to make the strongest possible assumption about the EPP in English: that *every* occurrence of T has a strong EPP feature. This analysis also allows us to analogize quotative inversion to locative inversion, where the PP moves into Spec TP position (as argued in chapter 2). For these two reasons (the EPP and the parallelism to locative inversion), I adopt this analysis in this chapter.

A third possibility is that the quote moves to Spec TP to check the EPP feature of T, then moves to Spec CP.[3] As far as I can see, the additional movement to Spec CP is consistent with my analysis in this chapter.

In the above discussion, I assumed that the quote itself moves to Spec TP. There is some evidence that it is not the quote that undergoes such movement, but rather an empty element (which I will call the *quotative operator*[4]). Consider the paradigm illustrated by (18).

(18)
a. "When on earth will the fishing begin?" asked Harry.
b. "When on earth," asked Harry, "will the fishing begin?"
c. Asked Harry: "When on earth will the fishing begin?"

Sentence (18a) is consistent with movement of the quote itself to Spec TP. However, (18b) shows that the quote may be discontinuous, and (18c) shows that the quote may appear to the right of the subject. If Spec TP in not discontinuous and is to the left of T′, the quote itself must not be in Spec TP in (18b) and (18c). Therefore, I assume, following Collins and Branigan 1995, that the quote itself is not in Spec TP; rather, the quote is coindexed with a null element in Spec TP.

We may assume that this element has no φ-features. Conceptually, this makes sense, since a quote could not be plural. Empirically, we know from (8) that the verb agrees with the post-verbal subject, which would be surprising if the quotative operator had φ-features and occupied Spec T. On the other hand, it is plausible to assume that the quotative operator is a nominal expression; thus, it makes sense to say that it has a D feature, which I will call D[quote]. I will return to the Case feature of the null operator in section 3.2.

Additional evidence that a null operator is involved in quotative inversion comes from the English sentences that behave syntactically and semantically very much like quotative inversion but have an overtly realized element, as illustrated in (19).

(19)
A: Mary stole the painting.
B: I told you so.
A: And so said John as well.

The element *so* is used to refer back to some earlier part of the discourse. In this sense it is semantically similar to the quotative operator in quotative inversion, which is coindexed with a quote. Syntactically, the element *so* triggers inversion of a main verb, just as a quotative operator triggers inversion. The fact that there is an overt element *so* that possesses several of the properties I have attributed to the quotative operator is evidence that there is a corresponding covert element in quotative inversion. (This evidence is discussed more extensively in Collins and Branigan 1995.)

The exact relationship between the quote and the rest of the sentence is in a quotative inversion construction remains in question. Following Collins and Branigan 1995, we may assume that the structure is analogous to a parenthetical construction, as illustrated in (20) (see McCawley 1982).

(20)
a. "John," said Mary, "wants to go to the store."
b. John, according to Mary, wants to go to the store.

In (20b), the constituent [according to Mary] is a parenthetical adverbial expression modifying the rest of the sentence. Similarly, it is plausible to assume that in (20a) [said Mary] is a parenthetical adverbial expression modifying the rest of the sentence. The difference between the two cases is that in quotative inversion an operator in Spec TP is coindexed with the quote.

3.1.4   Structural Conclusions about Quotative Inversion

I have now given evidence as to the positions of the subject, the verb, the quote and the quotative operator in a quotative inversion construction. To summarize, (22) shows the structure of (21).

(21)
"I am so happy," said Mary.

(22)

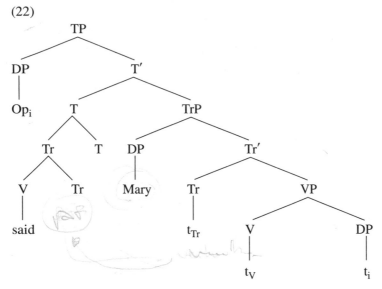

In this structure, the subject remains in Spec TrP. The verb has raised and adjoined to Tr, and Tr has raised and adjoined to T. The quotative operator is in Spec TP. Movement of the quotative operator satisfies Last Resort, since the quotative operator checks the EPP feature of T. At LF, the FF(Subj) (the formal features of Subj) raise and adjoin to T, accounting for the nominative Case of the post-verbal subject and the subject agreement on the verb.

Although I argued that the verb raises and adjoins to T in (22), I have yet to provide motivation for this movement. One relevant fact is that the verb whose complement is the quotative operator must raise to T (in other words, the verb introducing the direct speech complement), not any other verb. This is illustrated in (23).

(23)
a. "What time is it?" John was asking of Mona.
b. *"What time is it?" was John asking of Mona.
c. *"What time is it?" was asking John of Mona.

This paradigm shows that the auxiliary verb *was* may not raise to T in quotative inversion. As a consequence, quotative inversion seems to be impossible in the progressive aspect. Similarly, quotative inversion is impossible if *do*-support has occurred. This explains sentence (10f) above, repeated here as (24).

(24)
*"Let's eat," didn't John say just once

The generalization is that no auxiliary may raise to T in quotative inversion.[5] Lastly, if the verb whose complement is the quotative operator is an embedded verb (as in a control or raising construction), the matrix verb may not raise and adjoin to T in the quotative inversion construction, as illustrated in (25).

(25)
a. "Where is the puppy?" Essi wanted to know.
b. *"Where is the puppy?" wanted Essi to know.
c. *"Where is the puppy?" wanted to know Essi.

How can we account for these facts? Recall that I am assuming that there is a quotative operator that raises to Spec TP to check the strong EPP feature of T. I make the stipulation (26) to account for verb movement in quotative inversion.

(26)
The EPP feature of T may enter into a checking relation with the quotative operator only if V[Quote] adjoins to T.

The intuition behind this stipulation is that T must be supported by the actual quotative verb in order to check the D[quote] feature of the quotative operator. This movement for "support," which does not fit naturally into the framework of assumptions in chapter 2, is the only problematic stipulation in my theory. I expect that this kind of movement will become natural in a more articulated version of feature theory. I will not pursue the question of how to explain this stipulation any further here.[6]

3.2   Object Shift in Quotative Inversion

In this section, I will analyze further the movement of the quotative operator from the complement position in (22) to Spec TP. I will argue that the quote moves into the outer Spec TrP position to check both its Case feature and its D feature.

Consider first Case. In (22), the quotative operator is the complement of the verb *said*. Since the verb *say* usually has a Case feature to check, it should have one in this context as well. This entails that the quotative operator has a Case feature that must be checked. In fact there is evidence that the quotative operator has a Case feature that must be checked. Consider the paradigm illustrated in (27).

(27)
a. "John called us," Max said.
b. "John called us," was repeated over and over by Max.
c. *"John called us," it was repeated over and over by Max.

Sentence (27b) shows that the quotative operator can be (perhaps marginally) the subject of a tensed clause. Since T has a Case feature to check, it follows that the quotative operator must have a Case feature. Further evidence for this is given in (27c), where the quotative operator is moved from the complement position of the passive verb *repeated* (which has no Case feature to check). Since Spec T is occupied by *it* (which checks the Case feature of T), T has no Case feature to check either. Therefore, if the quotative operator has a Case feature, the sentence is predicted to be unacceptable, as is the case.

There are two ways in which the Case feature of the quotative operator could be checked in our framework. First, the Case feature could raise and adjoin to Tr at LF. Then the Case feature of the quotative operator would be in the checking domain of the accusative Case feature of Tr. Alternatively, the quotative operator could raise into the outer Spec Tr overtly. In essence, this would be an instance of overt object shift in English. I will argue for the latter alternative.

Now consider a related problem.[7] In the structure (22), movement of the quotative operator from the complement position to Spec TP has been postulated. (See subsection 3.1.5.) One problem with this movement is that it violates Minimality, repeated here as (28).

(28)
α can raise to a target K only if there is no operation (satisfying Last Resort) Move β targeting K, where β is closer to K.

In this case, K is T$'$, and α is the quotative operator, which raises to the target T$'$. The DP *Mary* in Spec Tr is closer to T$'$ than the quotative operator. To see this, consider again the diagram in (22). Note that *Mary* in the specifier of Tr is not in the same minimal domain as either the head or the tail of the operator chain. In addition, movement of *Mary* to Spec T would satisfy Last Resort, since *Mary* has a D feature that could check the EPP feature of T. Therefore, movement of the quotative operator to Spec T should be blocked by Minimality. Since it is not, it must be the case that the quotative operator is moving to an intermediate position that is allowing it to be as near to Spec T as the DP *Mary* in Spec Tr. A natural candidate for this position is the outside specifier of Tr.

We have assumed that the quotative operator has a special quotative determiner D[quote]. Let us suppose Tr (to which the quotative verb has adjoined) has a strong D feature that can be checked by a quotative operator. Under this assumption, the quotative operator may move to the outer Spec Tr to check the D feature.[8]

Given this movement, we can simultaneously resolve how the quotative operator checks its accusative Case feature. When the quotative operator moves to the outer Spec Tr, its Case feature will be in the checking domain of the Case feature of Tr. A checking relation is established, and both features are deleted (a case of symmetric feature checking).

Note that the quotative operator is a DP that has a Case feature, but no ϕ-features. This situation is anomalous in an Agr theory of clause structure. In such a theory, a DP moves to Spec Agr, where its Case and its ϕ-features enter into checking relations. If the DP does not have any ϕ-features, what sense does it make to say that it raises to the specifier of an agreement phrase?

Given this movement of the quotative operator, we will have the intermediate structure shown in (29).[9]

(29)

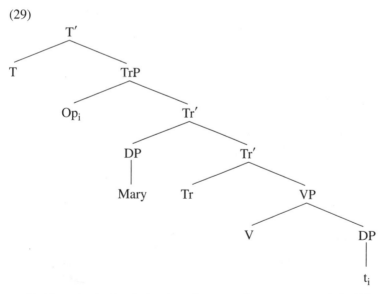

At this point in the derivation, the quotative operator and the DP *Mary* are in the minimal domain of the head Tr. Therefore, according to our definition of *closer* (see chapter 2), it follows that they are equidistant from T*. Therefore, either *Mary* or the quotative operator may raise and be merged with T′. In case the quotative operator moves, its D feature will check the EPP feature of T.

We are assuming that the D feature of the quotative operator checks both the D feature of Tr and the D feature of T. In other words, the single D feature of the quotative operator enters into two checking relations. This is not problematic from the standpoint of our theory, since asymmetric checking relations are allowed. In other words, when the D feature of the quotative operator enters into a checking relation with the D feature of the Tr the latter is deleted; however, the D feature of the quotative operator is not deleted, since it is an interpretable feature. Similarly, when the D feature of the quotative operator enters into a checking relation with the EPP feature of T only the latter is deleted. And when the quotative operator moves to Spec T, it does not check the Case feature of T, since the Case feature of the quotative operator has already been checked by Tr.

In the final step of the derivation, the Case and ϕ-features of the DP *Mary* (the FF(Mary)) in Spec Tr will raise and adjoin to T at LF. The Case feature of the subject will then be in the checking domain of T, accounting for the nominative Case found on the post-verbal subject in quotative inversion. The ϕ-features of the DP *Mary* will also be adjoined to T. These ϕ-features can be checked against the ϕ-features of the verb (which is adjoined to T overtly—see subsection 3.1.4).

There are several respects in which quotative inversion is parallel to locative inversion (see chapter 2) under my analysis. First, in each of these cases a constituent that does not receive nominative Case checks the EPP feature of T. In locative inversion, the PP raises into Spec T and checks the EPP feature of T. In quotative inversion, the quotative operator raises into Spec T and checks the EPP feature of T. Second, in each case inversion is made possible by the equidistance of a DP and some other constituent. In locative inversion, the DP in Spec VP and the PP complement of VP are equidistant, and so either may move. In quotative inversion, the quotative operator in the outer Spec Tr and the DP in the inner Spec Tr are equidistant, so either one may move.

The derivation of quotative inversion, which I shall call the inverted derivation, is summarized in (30).[10]

(30)
a. Op moves to outer specifier of Tr (the Case and D features of quotative operator enter into checking relations).
b. V raises and adjoins to Tr.
c. V raises and adjoins to T (the tense feature of the verb enters into a checking relation with T).
d. Op moves to Spec T (the EPP feature of T enters into a checking relation).
e. There is covert movement of FF(Subj) to adjoin to T (the Case and ϕ-features of subject enter into checking relations with the Case-assigning feature of T and the ϕ-features of the verb, respectively).

This derivation involves five movement operations. It also involves a number of pure Merge operations, which I do not indicate, since they are common to the inverted and non-inverted derivations. The operator moves twice, there are two overt head movements (the V raises and adjoins to Tr; Tr raises and adjoins to T), and the features FF(Subj) raise and adjoin to T at LF.

In the next section, I will consider the alternative non-inverted derivation where the quotative operator does not move into Spec TP. I will show that this derivation involves fewer steps than the inverted derivation. Even before analyzing the non-inverted derivation, it should be intuitively clear that it will be shorter than the inverted derivation. Just as in the case of locative inversion, the inverted derivation involves a "wasteful" movement: movement of the quotative operator into Spec T checks only the EPP feature of T and not the Case feature of T. Therefore, a comparison of the two derivations is highly relevant to the discussion of local economy.

3.3 Local Economy and Quotative Inversion

Now consider the derivation involving no inversion. In other words, assume the derivation has reached the point where the Op has moved to Spec Tr (to check the strong D feature of Tr), and either the Op or the DP in Spec Tr is able to move to Spec TP. I repeat a diagram of this point of the derivation as (31).

(31)

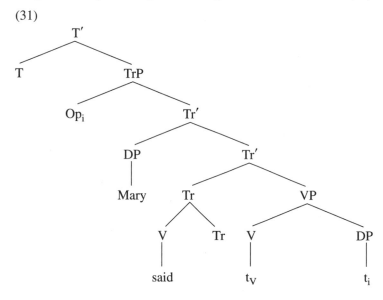

Now suppose that the DP *Mary* moves to Spec TP, and that it checks the EPP feature of T and the Case feature of T simultaneously. Movement of the verb proceeds in two steps. Overtly, the verb moves and adjoins to Tr. This verb movement is common to the inverted and non-inverted derivations. At LF, Tr (or simply its formal features) raises and adjoins to T. At this point, the φ-features of the verb are checked against the φ-feature of the DP *Mary* in Spec TP. There is no need to raise the verb and the Tr to T overtly, since the EPP feature of T is not being checked by the quotative operator (see subsection 3.1.4). This derivation is summarized in (32).

(32)
a. Op moves to outer Spec of Tr (the Case and D features of quotative operator enter into checking relations).
b. V raises and adjoins to Tr.
c. Subj moves to Spec T (the Case and EPP features of T enter into checking relations).
d. Tr raises and adjoins to T covertly (the φ-features of subject enter into a checking relation with the φ-features of the verb, and the tense feature of the verb enters into a checking relation with T).

This derivation takes four steps. The operator moves a single time. There are two instances of head movement (the V raises and adjoins to Tr overtly, and Tr raises and adjoins to T covertly). The DP *Mary* raises to Spec T and checks the Case and EPP feature of T simultaneously. Therefore, the non-inverted derivation is less costly than the inverted derivation by one step.

At this point it is instructive to analyze more closely the additional step found in the inverted derivation. Each derivation involves two head movements, so the two factor out. Each involves the Op moving from the complement position of the verb to Spec Tr, so these movements also factor out. The fundamental difference between the inverted and the non-inverted derivation is that in the non-inverted derivation the EPP feature of T and the Case feature of T are checked as the result of one movement operation (the DP moves to Spec T). On the other hand, in the inverted derivation the checking of the EPP feature of T and the Case feature of T is distributed across two movements. This is analogous to the difference we found between inverted and non-inverted derivations for locative inversion.

We conclude from this comparison that there can be no global economy condition such as the Shortest Derivation Requirement of chapter 1 (which states that the number of operations needed for convergence should be minimized). To see this, note first that both the inverted and the non-inverted derivation have the same lexical items, so there is no strong reason to assume that the Numerations for these two derivations are different.[11] Given that the Numerations are the same, the inverted and non-inverted derivations are in the same reference set. Therefore, if the SDR held, it would block quotative inversion, contrary to fact. On the other hand, both of the derivations above satisfy the local economy conditions of Minimality and Last Resort at every step in the derivation. Therefore, the existence of such inversion phenomena suggests that economy conditions are local.

An alternative solution that retains global economy is the following. Consider again the inverted derivation in (30). This derivation has five movement operations. If we could reduce the number of movement operations by one, then it would have four movement operations, and the inverted and non-inverted derivations would have the same number of operations. One way to reduce the number of movement operations in the inverted derivation is to collapse steps (30a) and (30c) into one operation of Form Chain. In other words, the quotative operator undergoes movement from the complement position of the verb to Spec Tr, and then undergoes a further movement from Spec Tr to Spec TP. If we could join these two movements together into one operation of Form Chain, we would have the derivation shown in (33).[12]

(33)
a. Form Chain: Op moves to outer specifier of Tr and subsequently Op moves to Spec T.
b. V raises and adjoins to Tr.
c. V raises and adjoins to T.
d. There is covert movement of FF(Subj) to adjoin to T.

Although the use of Form Chain makes the inverted derivation have the same number of movement operations as the non-inverted derivation, we will see in chapter 5 that there is little reason to postulate an operation of Form Chain. Once Last Resort is defined to allow each step of successive cyclic movement, Form Chain becomes superfluous. Therefore, I reject this solution.

My derivation of quotative inversion is analogous to Ura's (1996) derivation of inversion in Bantu (also called "subject-object reversal"). Inversion in Bantu is illustrated in (34).[13]

(34)
a. Mutu   t-a-ku-sol-ag-a   maku   weneene
   1person   neg-1-prog-drink-hab-fv   6beer   alone
   "A person does not usually drink beer alone."
b. Maku   ta-ma-ku-sol-ag-a   mutu   weneene
   6beer   neg-6-prog-drink-hab-fv   1person   alone
   "Beer is not usually drunk by a person alone."

Ura (1996) notes several properties of inversion. First, the normal word order of Bantu is SVO, as illustrated in (34a). In Kilega, as in all Bantu languages, there is agreement of the verb with the subject. In (34a), the subject is in the first noun class, and this agrees with the verb. In the inversion in (34b), the DP *maku* "beer" appears before the verb, and the verb is followed by *mutu* "person." In addition, the subject agreement on the verb is with *maku* "beer" and not with *mutu* "person." The agreement on the verb is the strongest evidence that there has been inversion of the subject and the object (there is no overt morphological Case on the DPs to indicate their grammatical relations).

Inversion is different from passive, in that there is no morpheme that is used in forming inversion (whereas there is a passive morpheme in Bantu languages). In addition, the agent is not "demoted" to appear in a prepositional phrase in inversion.

Ura (1996) gives the following analysis of inversion (the analysis is modified a little to make it conform to the assumptions of chapter 2). Ura assumes that the D feature of Tr is strong in Kilega (and other languages allowing inversion), that the Case feature of T is weak, and that the EPP feature of T is strong (Ura assumes that the verb always raises to T in Kilega). As the underlying structure we have (35).

(35)

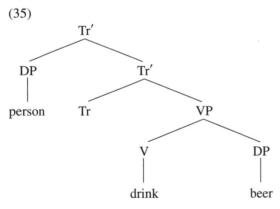

Since the D feature of Tr is strong, the complement DP may undergo object shift. At this point the Case feature of *maku* "beer" is in the checking domain of the Case feature of Tr. Therefore, we may assume that a checking relation is established, and both features delete. This movement yields (36).

(36)

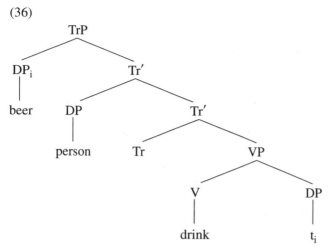

At this point in the derivation, either DP *maku* "beer" or the DP *mutu* "person" may raise into Spec T. Since both DPs are in the minimal domain of the Tr, neither one is closer to T. In the inverted derivation (leading to (34b)), movement of *maku* "beer" to Spec TP satisifies Last Resort, since its D feature checks the strong EPP feature of T (but not the Case feature of T) and its ϕ-features check the class 6 ϕ-features on the verb. At LF, the Case feature of *mutu* "person" raises and adjoins to T and enters into a checking relation with the weak Case feature of T.

Now consider the non-inverted derivation starting from the structure in (36). In the non-inverted derivation (leading to (34a)) *mutu* "person" raises to Spec T; it checks both the EPP feature and the Case feature of T at the same time, and it checks the class 1 ϕ-features on the verb.

Because the inverted and non-inverted derivations have different agreement patterns, inversion in Bantu is not directly equivalent to quotative inversion, where the inverted and non-inverted derivations have the same agreement patterns (agreement is always with the agent, or the DP in Spec Tr). However, inversion in Bantu does show how the general derivation that I postulated for quotative inversion is cross-linguistically attested; this adds plausibility to my analysis.

3.4   The Transitivity Constraint

Perhaps the most interesting restriction on quotative inversion is the transitivity constraint. Quotative inversion may never occur with a double object verb, as illustrated by (37) and (38).

(37)

a. "I am so happy," Mary said to John.

b. "I am so happy," said Mary to John.

(38)

a. "I am so happy," Mary told John.

b. *"I am so happy," told Mary John.

These examples show that the verb *say* allows quotative inversion, but not the verb *tell*. The difference between these two verbs is that *tell* takes both an indirect object and a direct object, whereas *say* takes a direct object and a PP complement. A similar contrast can be found with the verb *ask*, as illustrated by (39) and (40).

(39)

a. "What is the exchange rate?" Mary asked of John.

b. "What is the exchange rate?" asked Mary of John.

(40)

a. "What is the exchange rate?" Mary asked John.

b. *"What is the exchange rate?" asked Mary John.

As shown in (39), when the verb *ask* takes a direct object and a PP complement, quotative inversion is allowed. On the other hand, as shown in (40), when *ask* takes an indirect object and a direct object, quotative inversion is not allowed.

The generalization seems to be that quotative inversion is not allowed with double object verbs. Therefore, in order to understand this effect, we must have a theory of Case checking in double object constructions. I will adapt the theory of Collins and Thráinsson 1993 and Collins and Thráinsson 1995 to the present framework.[14]

3.4.1 A Review of Collins and Thráinsson 1993 and 1995

In order to account for the transitivity constraint on quotative inversion, we must have some account of Case checking in double object constructions. Consider (41).

(41)

John gave Mary the ball.

What is the structure of the double object construction? What head checks the Case feature of *Mary*? What head checks the Case feature of *the ball*? If object shift is analyzed as movement of a DP to a Case-checking position, then how does object shift work in double object constructions (where there are two DPs, each with a Case feature to check)? All these questions are addressed in Collins and Thráinsson 1993 and in Collins and Thráinsson 1995, where object shift in double object constructions in Icelandic is analyzed. This theory was presented in terms of the Agr theory of clause structure. I will review this theory briefly, and then show how it may be easily translated into a multiple-specifier theory.

As I mentioned in chapter 2, object shift in Icelandic is driven by Case checking (and by checking of the D feature of Tr). Consider the following example of object shift in Icelandic, repeated from chapter 2:

(42)
a. Jón   las   bækurnar   ekki.
   John   read   the books   not
   "John did not read the books."
b. Jón   las   ekki   bækurnar.
   John   read   not   the books
   "John did not read the books."

In (42a), the object has shifted to the left of an adverb (which we may assume is adjoined to Tr′). In Collins and Thráinsson 1993 and in Collins and Thráinsson 1995 this is analyzed as movement of the object to Spec Agr$_O$. In this position, the Case feature of the object is checked against the verb, and the ϕ-features of the object are checked against Agr$_O$. This analysis is illustrated in (43).

(43)

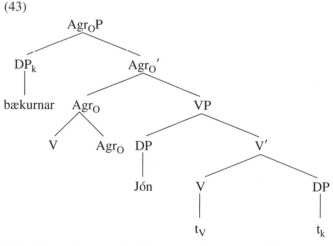

With this analysis, and with the locality theory of Chomsky 1993 (adopted by Collins and Thráinsson (1993, 1995)), the analysis of object shift in double object constructions poses a problem, each DP should block the other from getting to a Case position.

As was shown in Collins and Thráinsson 1993 and in Collins and Thráinsson 1995, if a VP-internal Agr$_O$P projection and a VP-internal TP projection were assumed, the problem of object shift in double object constructions could be solved. Consider a derivation in which both objects of a double object verb are shifted, as in (44).[15]

(44)
?Ég   lána   Maríu   bækurnar   ekki.
I   lend   Maria   the books   not
"I do not lend Maria the books."

In this example both the indirect object and the direct object are to the left of negation. (Negation may appear in the sentence-final position only if there has been an object shift.) With a VP-internal Agr projection and a VP-internal TP projection postulated, the structure of (44) was given by Collins and Thráinsson as follows:

(45)

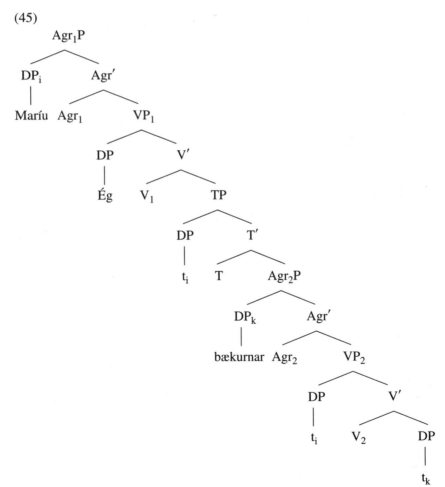

In this structure there are two VP "shells."[16] The lower VP_2 projection is where the indirect object and the direct object are generated. The upper VP_1 projection introduces the external argument. The upper V_1 checks the Case of the indirect object, which moves to Spec Agr_1. The Case of the direct object is checked by V_2, when the direct object moves to Spec Agr_2. I leave out a representation of the relevant head movement for simplicity. Under the locality theory of Chomsky (1993), the inner TP is needed to allow the indirect object to move to Spec Agr_1.

The derivation proceeds as follows: (1) The verb *lend* adjoins to Agr_2. The chain thus formed renders Spec VP_2 (the base position of the indirect object) and Spec Agr_2 equidistant from the complement of V_2. The object then moves into Spec Agr_2, skipping Spec VP_2. (2) Agr_2 adjoins to the embedded T, rendering Spec Agr_2 and Spec TP equidistant from Spec VP_2. The indirect object then moves to Spec TP, skipping Spec Agr_2. (3) The embedded T adjoins to V_1, and the complex V_1 adjoins to Agr_1. This renders Spec VP_1 and Spec Agr_1 equidistant from the embedded Spec TP. The indirect object then moves from the Spec of the embedded TP to Spec Agr_1. (4) Agr_1 adjoins to the matrix T, rendering Spec Agr_1 and Spec TP equidistant from Spec VP_1 (the base position of the subject). The subject then raises from Spec VP_1 to the Spec of the matrix TP, skipping Spec Agr_1.

Under the assumptions of Chomsky (1993), the above analysis was pretty much the unique solution available to the problem of object shift in double object constructions. Unsurprisingly, many aspects of the above analysis translate into the framework in chapter 2.

3.4.2 Object Shift in Double Object Constructions

Let us now consider how we can translate this analysis into our current framework (see Ura 1996 for a similar proposal). The essential part of the analysis is that the Case of the indirect object is checked by V_1 and the Case of the direct object is checked by V_2.

First, the upper VP shell (VP_1) has been replaced by Tr (transitivity) in the current framework. It was suggested in Collins and Thráinsson 1995 that the lower VP shell (V_2) could be decomposed into an applicative affix and a lexical verb (following roughly Marantz 1993). The applicative affix serves two functions: it introduces the indirect object (just as Tr introduces the external argument), and it checks the case of the direct object (just as Tr checks the case of the indirect object). I assume (for convenience) that the category of Appl is V, so it projects a VP.

In summary, we need to eliminate the Agr phrases, replace V_1 by Tr, and decompose V_2 into an applicative affix and a lexical verb. In addition, we can eliminate the VP-internal TP projection. In the system of Collins and Thráinsson 1993 and Collins and Thráinsson 1995, the principal function of the VP-internal TP projection was to allow both objects to shift without violating the locality theory of Chomsky 1993 (basically Relativized Minimality augmented with equidistance defined in terms of head chains). In the system of locality that I have adopted here, the function of TP is superfluous. Since there is no other strong motivation for the VP-internal TP projection, I will simply not represent it in further diagrams. If it turns out that later some additional evidence is found for the VP-internal TP projection, it can be added to my analysis without problem.

These modifications yield the structure shown in (46) (where no object shift has taken place).

(46)

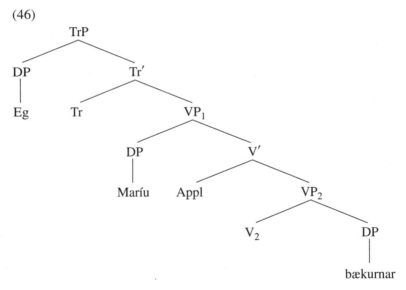

This structure maintains the essence of the analysis of Collins and Thráinsson 1993 and Collins and Thráinsson 1995 in that there are two heads (Tr and Appl), each of which is responsible for the Case of one DP. This structure is clearly simpler than the structure in (45). Below, I will show that it can handle the facts about object shift in a similar way.

I will now illustrate the derivation where both objects are shifted. Assume that the VP_2 projection has already been constructed through a series of Merge operations. In addition, the complement of the verb has been raised to the outside specifier position of V_1. This yields the structure shown in (47).

(47)

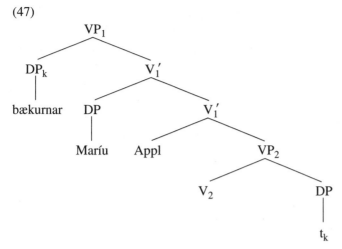

The movement of the DP *bækurnar* "the books" does not violate Minimality. The DP *Maríu* and the DP *bækurnar* "the books" are in the same minimal domain (of Appl), and therefore the DP *Maríu* does not block movement of the DP *bækurnar* "the books." Next, the hcad Tr is Merged into the structure, then the specifier of Tr. This yields the structure shown in (48).

(48)

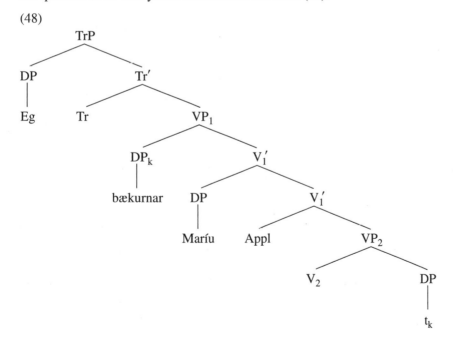

The DP *Maríu* now undergoes raising to the outer specifier of TrP. Neither the shifted direct object DP *bækurnar* "the books" nor the *in situ* subject DP *Ég* "I" will block the movement of the DP *Maríu*. The shifted direct object DP *bækurnar* "the books" and the DP *Maríu* are in the minimal domain of Appl, and therefore the shifted direct object is not closer to the outer specifier of Tr than the indirect object. Similarly, the outer specifier of Tr and the DP *Ég* "I" in the inner specifier of Tr are in the minimal domain of the same Tr head, and so the DP *Ég* "I" is not closer to the outer specifier of Tr than the indirect object. The raising of the indirect object yields the structure shown in (49).

(49)

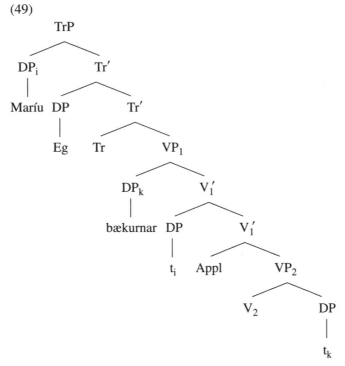

In summary, we have seen how the locality theory (Minimality in chapter 2) that we are adopting combines with our assumptions about clause structure (no Agr projections) to yield an account of object shift in double object constructions.

In Collins and Thráinsson 1993 and Collins and Thráinsson 1995 a number of constraints on object shift in double object constructions were analyzed. Perhaps the most important of these is that if both an indirect object and a direct object have undergone object shift then the order cannot change.[17] This is illustrated by (50).

(50)

a. *Ég   lána   bækurnar   Maríu   ekki.
   I   lend   the books   Maria   not
   "I do not lend the books to Maria."

Collins and Thráinsson show that, under their assumptions, the derivation of this sentence involves a violation of locality.[18] It is easy to see that the same insight carries over into the set of assumptions discussed in chapter 2. Consider (51), which shows what the structure of (50) would be in the multiple-specifier theory.

(51)

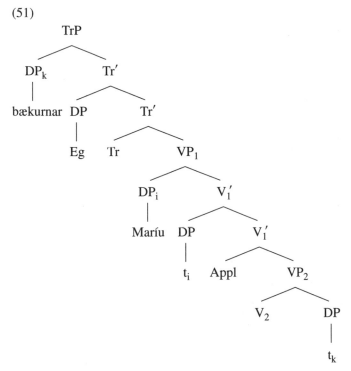

In this structure, the DP *bækurnar* "the books" has moved from the complement position of the verb V_2 to the outer spec of Tr to check the D feature and the Case feature of Tr. This movement is prohibited by Minimality. The DP *Maríu* is not in the same minimal domain as either the head or the tail of the chain ([*bækurnar*]$_k$, t_k). Therefore, the DP *Maríu* is closer to the outer specifier of Tr than the DP *bækurnar* "the books." In addition, the movement of *Maríu* to the outer specifier of Tr would satisfy Last Resort, since the D feature of Tr could check the D feature of *Maríu*. Therefore, the movement of the DP *bækurnar* "the books" to the outer specifier of Tr is blocked.

3.4.3   Analysis of the Transitivity Constraint

Given this overview of the structure of the double object constructions, an analysis of the transitivity constraint on quotative inversion is readily in hand. The examples illustrating the transitivity constraint are repeated in (52).

(52)
a. "I am so happy," Mary told John.
b. *"I am so happy," told Mary John.

Since *tell* is a double object verb, the structure of (52b) will be as shown in (53).[19]

(53)

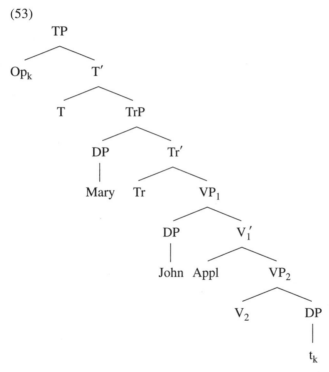

This movement violates Minimality. There are two DPs (*Mary* and *John*) that are closer to T′ than the *in situ* position of the quotative operator. Each of the DPs has a D feature that could check the EPP feature of T. Therefore, these DPs would block the movement of the quotative operator to Spec TP.

Recall that we have postulated that in quotative constructions, Tr has a strong D[quote] feature that can trigger movement of the quotative operator. If we continue to make this assumption, we will have the structure shown in (54).

(54)

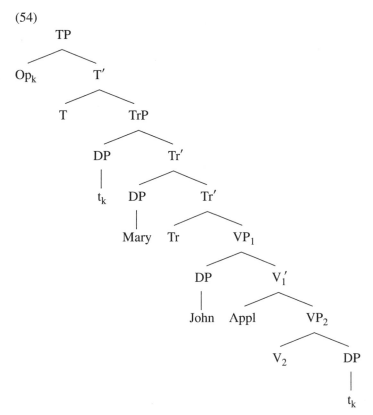

This structure violates Minimality. Although the DP *Mary* presents no problem (since it is in the same minimal domain as the outer specifier position of Tr), the DP *John* blocks movement of the quotative operator. The DP *John* is closer to the outer specifier of Tr than the *in situ* position of the quotative operator, and it has a D feature that could check the D feature of Tr.

In discussing (54) we assumed that Tr has a strong D[quote] feature, on analogy with quotative inversion in regular transitive verbs. However, in double object constructions there are two functional heads that could in principle have a strong D[quote] feature: Tr and Appl. Given this, consider now the possibility that Appl has the strong D[quote] feature that triggers movement of the quotative operator. This assumption would give rise to the structure shown in (55).

(55)

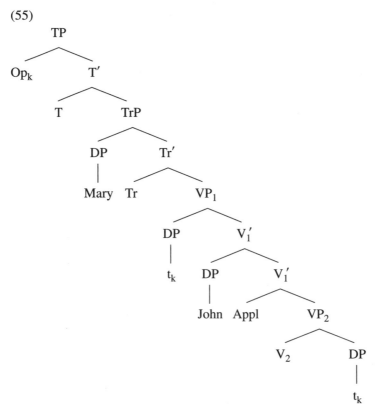

In this structure, the DP *John* does not block movement of the quotative operator, since it is in the same minimal domain as the outer specifier of Appl. The
problematic DP is *Mary*, which is closer to Spec T than the outer specifier of
Appl and which has a D feature that can check the EPP feature of T.

So far I have shown that, regardless of whether Tr has a strong D[quote]
feature, or Appl has a strong D[quote] feature, movement of the quotative operator to Spec T cannot occur. There is one more possibility that we must investigate: the possibility that both Tr and Appl have strong D[quote] features,
and that these features trigger movement of the quotative operator to both the
outer specifier of Appl and the outer specifier of Tr. It is easy to verify that this
would allow the quotative operator to move to Spec T to check the EPP feature
of T (I leave it to the reader to perform this calculation). Therefore, if both Tr
and Appl could have a strong D[quote] feature, we would falsely predict that
quotative inversion would be possible with double object verbs.

There are several ways to block this derivation. If the D[quote] feature were to be restricted to the head that also checked the Case feature of the quotative operator, then the strong D[quote] feature would have to be restricted to Appl alone, since Appl checks the Case of the quotative operator (and, more generally, the direct object in a double object construction). The head Tr, on the other hand, checks the Case feature of the indirect object. Why this restriction should hold is not clear at the moment.

A more plausible approach is to limit the number of D[quote] features that can appear on the functional heads dominating a quotative verb to one. In that case, either Tr or Appl will have the D[quote] feature, but not both.

3.5   Conclusion

In this chapter, I have given an analysis of quotative inversion where a quotative operator moves to Spec T and satisfies the EPP feature of T. As we have seen, the inverted derivation involves more steps than the non-inverted derivation. Given global economy and the Shortest Derivation Requirement, we may expect quotative inversion to be blocked. However, they are not blocked; this suggests that local economy is more adequate to explaining the facts about locative inversion and quotative inversion.

I have also shown how an adaptation of the theory of double object constructions to the framework of Chomsky 1995 and Ura 1996 yields the straightforward prediction that quotative inversion cannot occur with ditransitive verbs.

One unsatisfactory aspect of the argument against global economy based on locative inversion and quotative inversion is that the operations that make one derivation longer than another are covert. For both types of inversion, the reason why the inverted derivation in longer is that it involves LF movement of FF(DP) to adjoin to T. Although this is a good start, a definitive argument against global economy would involve a case where all the operations are overt. I will leave the discovery of examples of this type to future work.[20]

Chapter 4

Phrase Structure

In this chapter I will examine some of the implications of local economy for the theory of phrase structure. I will show how Last Resort may be extended to Merge, by introducing a condition which I call Integration; how binary branching may be looked at as the result of Minimality, given a certain construal of Merge; and how the strict cycle reduces to Kayne's (1994) Linear Correspondence Axiom, and how this result is related to local economy. Also, I will give preliminary consideration to the elimination of the concept of Numeration. The final argument for eliminating the Numeration will be presented in chapter 5.

The results of this chapter, which are more abstract than those of chapters 2 and 3, serve to show the wide-ranging implications that local economy can have for the form of grammar.

4.1 The Definition of Merge

One fact about language is that words are grouped in larger phrases. In generative grammar this fact has been captured by X′ theory, as illustrated in (1).

(1)
a. XP → YP X′   (order irrelevant)
b. X′ → X ZP   (order irrelevant)

These kinds of constraints combine many types of information: The grouping of X and ZP, and of X′ and YP, is encoded. The level of projection is encoded. The category of the projections involved is encoded. The binary branching nature of projections is also encoded.

Assuming that all the information in (1) is necessary,[1] we can ask if the formulation given there is the simplest. To address this question, consider (2), which illustrates the simplest way to represent the grouping of two constituents, α and β.

(2)
Merge(α,β) = {α,β}.

There are two reasons why such a representation might not be sufficient[2]: the head of the derived constituent {α,β} is not represented in (2), and this representation does not allow the distinction between segments and categories.

There are many reasons for assuming that the notion of head plays a role in grammatical theory. One is that it plays a role in locality theory, where the head of constituent can undergo movement to a higher head (part of the Head Movement Constraint (Travis 1984)). The notion of head also plays a role in θ theory, where the head of a VP assigns a θ-role to its complement. In view of these considerations, the minimal assumption is that there is a function that, given a constituent, yields a head[3]:

(3)
If α is minimal, Head(α) = α; otherwise, Head({α,β}) = Head(α).

The idea here is that the choice of the head is defined recursively (we will assume that finding the head is not an operation, so it is not economized). To find the head of a constituent, one simply finds the head of one of its daughters. I will assume that the head of a constituent is calculated automatically at the time the constituent is formed by Merge. In addition, I will assume that the head cannot be changed during the derivation.[4]

To see how this constituent structure works, consider (4), where Σ and the Numeration N are omitted for simplicity.

(4)
i.   Select V
ii.   Select N
iii. Merge(N, V) = {N, V}
      Head({N,V}) = V
iv.   Select Agr_O
v.   Merge(Agr_O, {N, V}) = {Agr_O, {N, V}}
      Head({Agr_O, {N,V}}) = Agr_O.

Suppose that at step (4iii) the N was chosen as head instead of V. Then at LF we would have a NP with a VP complement. It is reasonable to assume that the V will be uninterpretable in this situation. (In other words, V can assign a θ-role to N only if N is a specifier or complement of V.)

Consider the case of Move. If Move takes β and a copy of α, and merges them, we obtain the structure Merge(α,β) = {α,β}. In the case of Move, Chomsky (1994:

400) argues that it is always the target that projects. If Move targets β and Moves α, then β must project. This is represented in our system as $\text{Head}(\{\alpha,\beta\}) = \beta$.

The second problem with the representation in (2) is that it does not allow for the distinction between segments and categories. In other words, if we suppose that β is the head of structure, how can we determine from (2) whether α is adjoined to β, or whether α and β are merged to form a new category? We may ask how adjunction can be defined in such a sparse representation. Chomsky (1994: 402) proposes that to minimally distinguish a segment from a category we use the notion of ordered pair.[5] Adding this idea to our assumptions, we have (5).

(5)
Merge$(\alpha, \beta) = \{\alpha, \beta\}$ (non-adjunction)
Merge$(\alpha, \beta) = \{\alpha, \langle\beta,\beta\rangle\}$ (adjunction of α to β)

This definition of adjunction captures the fact that, if α is adjoined to β, then α is a daughter of $\{\alpha, \langle\beta,\beta\rangle\}$ but β is not.[6] Rather, the two daughters of the adjoined structure are α and a segment of β, which is $\langle\beta,\beta\rangle$. In order to complete this definition we need only (6).

(6)
$\text{Head}(\langle\beta,\beta\rangle) = \text{Head}(\beta)$.

Is the definition of Head in the above paragraphs minimalist in spirit? The question to ask is whether there is any minimal theory of grammar that would not have this definition and whether a theory of grammar that did not have this definition was a notational variant. This seems improbable.

4.2   Integration

In the minimalist program a derivation is viewed as a mapping from a Numeration to a pair (PF, LF). The Numeration is defined as a set of pairs (LI, i), where LI is a lexical item and i is the index that tells how many times LI is to be selected from the Numeration. An element LI in the Numeration is selected (by the operation Select) from the Numeration (reducing its index by one). Once selected, the lexical item is merged with one of the syntactic objects in Σ. This series of operations (Select followed by Merge) constitutes lexical insertion. I will reevaluate these assumptions in section 4.6.

Is the process of lexical insertion subject to economy? It is not obvious that it should be: if it were, it is not clear that sentences could even be formed (since they would involve costly lexical insertions). On the other hand, the minimal assumption is that lexical insertion and the Merge operation that underlies it should be subject to economy. The minimal assumption is that *all* operations are subject to economy, unless there is overwhelming evidence to the contrary. In this section, I will show how there is a natural way of viewing Merge as being subject to economy.

Consider the sentence *John left* and the (partial) derivation shown in (7).

(7)
i.   Select John.
ii. Select left.
iii. Merge(John, left) = {John, left}.

What motivates the Merge operation in step (7iii)? It is not clear what feature of either *John* or *left* is being checked by the operation in step (7iii), so it seems as if this step violates Last Resort. One possibility (which I will reject) is that one property of *John* that must be satisfied is that *John* must be taken out of the Numeration (in other words, *John* must be selected, and its integer in the Numeration is reduced by one). This property is satisfied by steps (7ii) and (7iii), and therefore those steps do not violate Last Resort.

I will assume that in steps (7i) and (7ii) Select does not have to be motivated (in other words, it is not subject to Last Resort). Select is not really an operation; rather, it can be seen as a part (or a reflex) of the operation Merge or Move. In other words, whenever Select takes place, it is followed by Merge. Therefore, we can view Merge as a complex operation consisting of Merge and Select. (See section 4.6 for more discussion of this issue.)

However, the property that a lexical item must be taken out of the Numeration does not generalize. If we have two phrases that have been built by applications of Merge, say α and β, merging these two phrases cannot be motivated by a condition involving the Numeration, since neither α nor β was in the numeration.

A closely related alternative is to assume that Merge of α and β (whether lexical or not) is driven by the fact that both α and β must be integrated into the clause. Therefore, Merge may be considered to be motivated, but not by feature checking. I call this condition *Integration*, and define it as in (8).

(8)
Every category (except the root) must be contained in another category.[7]

This is a syntactic property of every constituent, lexical or not. It does not obviously follow from any semantic requirement. It could be considered one of the defining properties of the notion constituent. Every constituent must be a daughter of some other constituent (except the root).

If Integration is a property that Merge satisfies, Last Resort must be generalized in an appropriate way. In chapter 2, where I discussed locative and quotative inversion, I defined Last Resort as in (9).

(9)
Move raises α to the checking domain of a head H with a feature F only if the feature F of H enters into a checking relation with a feature F of α.

Clearly this condition is not relevant for Integration, since Integration does not make reference to features. Therefore, the formulation of Last Resort in (9) is overly restrictive. Last Resort should make reference to any property that is relevant to the internal operations of the syntactic computation. One of these properties happens to be feature checking; another happens to be dominance. Given this consideration, consider the extension of Last Resort shown as (10).

(10)
An operation OP involving α may apply only if some property of α is satisfied.

As part of the definition of Last Resort, the relevant properties must be specified. In the case of Merge, the relevant property is Integration. In the case of Move, the relevant property of α is that a feature of α must enter into a checking relation (where checking relation is defined as in chapter 2).[8] This feature-checking relation could be asymmetric, as will be discussed in chapter 5.

The condition of Integration is clearly related to the Linear Correspondence Axiom (LCA) of Kayne (1994: 6). If a phrase is not integrated into a clause, its terminals will not be ordered with respect to the other terminals. The LCA is stated in (11).

(11)   *Linear Correspondence Axiom*
d(A) is a linear ordering of T.

In this definition, T is the set of terminals, A is the set of pairs of nonterminals (X, Y) such that X asymmetrically c-commands Y, and d is a mapping of A to a set of ordered pairs of terminals (for further details see Kayne 1994). If some category XP (in addition to the root) is not contained in another category, then there will be some terminal dominated by XP that is not in d(A). Although Integration and LCA are clearly related, I will not attempt to derive Integration from LCA here.[9] The basic reason is as follows: Kayne (1995, chapter 2) argues that the principles of $\overline{\text{X}}$ theory follow from the LCA. From this, Kayne (ibid.: 48) concludes the LCA applies at all levels (D-Structure, S-Structure, LF)—or, in a theory without these levels, to all intermediate representations. On the other hand, Chomsky (1994) argues that all the basic assumptions of $\overline{\text{X}}$ theory follow from minimal assumptions about Merge and from the definition of maximal and minimal projection. Therefore, Chomsky abandons Kayne's conclusion that $\overline{\text{X}}$ theory is derived from LCA, while retaining the LCA as a condition following Spell-Out.

In view of Chomsky's (1994) formulation of the LCA, it is now clear that Integration (which applies at every step in the derivation) may not be derived from the LCA, although it has a clear conceptual relation to it. From now on, I will assume that the two conditions are independent.

Looking at Merge as being motivated by Integration in this way can provide an answer to the question of why derivation (12) is chosen over derivation (13).

(12)
i.   Select John.
ii. Select left.
iii. Merge(John, left) = {John, left}.

(13)
Do nothing (no operations).

Intuitively, the sequence of operations (zero operations) in (13) is less costly than the sequence of operations in (12). However, given Integration and local economy, there is no difference in cost between the derivations. Step (12iii) satisfies Integration, and the two Select operations are free (being parts of the Merge operation). Therefore, just as (13) satisfies economy, so does (12), and both derivations are allowed.

An alternative global way of looking at the difference between (12) and (13) is worth discussing. Chomsky (1994: 393) suggests that the computation does not converge unless all the elements in the Numeration have been selected (and their indices have been reduced to zero). In addition, in Chomsky 1994 some economy conditions like Procrastinate only select the optimal derivation among the set of convergent derivations, thus forcing overt movement of X if no convergent derivation exists with covert movement of X. Under these assumptions, the derivation (12) would be selected over that of (13), since (13) is not convergent (even if (13) is less costly). I reject this for the reason that restricting the set of derivations from which economy chooses the optimal derivation to the set of convergent derivations is global, as discussed in chapter 1. (See Chomsky 1995: 221 for a global analysis along these lines.)

To clarify what is being proposed, consider (14), where lexical insertion and movement compete locally.

(14)
a. A man is in the room.
b. There is a man in the room.

From a global perspective, the derivations of these two sentences do not compete, since they do not have the same Numeration. As will be pointed out in section 4.6, the Numeration may be eliminated with local economy. Therefore, let us see how local economy allows the two sentences above. The crucial step in the derivation is after [$_{T'}$ is a man in the room] has been formed. At that step there are two possible operations. First, *there* may be inserted, yielding (14b). This satisfies Last Resort, since the Integration property of *there* is satisfied. Second, *a man* may be raised to Spec T. This satisfies Last Resort, since both the EPP and Case features of T enter a checking relation. Therefore, locally both derivations are allowed, and both sentences are acceptable.

An important consequence of this reasoning is that there is no way that lexical insertion and pure Merge are less costly than movement (or Copy + Merge). This consequence will play an important role in chapter 6, where Procrastinate will be examined in more detail.

Looking at Merge as being motivated by Integration makes it possible to explain an asymmetry between Move (binary GT) and Merge (unary GT). Consider the derivation (15) (from Chomsky 1994: 401).

(15)
John [t HIT t]

Why is there no verb HIT that has no Case to assign to its object while at the same time assigning two θ-roles (an agent and a patient)? Such a HIT would participate in the derivation (16).

(16)
i.   Select John.
ii. Select HIT.
iii. Merge(John, HIT) = {John, HIT}.
iv. Copy John.
v.   Merge(John, {John, HIT}) = {John, {John, HIT}}.

In other words, why can't *John* raise to a θ-position? The answer to this question is that movement of *John* to a θ-position would not result in the checking of any feature of *John* or of the *verb HIT*, and so the movement fails by Last Resort.[10]

If θ-role assignment is a form of feature checking, then the derivation in (16) should be allowed, since movement of *John* into the specifier of *HIT* would satisfy Last Resort. The conclusion that θ-role assignment is not feature checking is strongly supported on conceptual grounds. Such assignment is a form of interpretation, properly conceived of as part of the syntax-semantics interface.

Thus, it makes no sense to verify whether θ-role assignment has been satisfied at an intermediate step in the derivation; that would make as much sense as asking what the reference of the word *dog* is at an intermediate step in the derivation. There is a parallel with phonology here. Just as phonological properties do not seem to influence syntactic computations, semantic properties (such as θ-roles and their assignment) should not be assumed to influence syntactic computations unless there is overwhelming evidence to the contrary.

Blocking movement into a θ-position by Last Resort seems problematic in light of step (12iii). Why can an argument be merged (pure Merge) into a θ-position but not moved into a θ-position. The difference is that in the case of movement there is no motivation to raise into a θ-position, whereas with lexical insertion the Integration property itself is a motivation.[11]

This assumption that θ-role assignment is not feature checking plays a role in another argument for local economy. Consider (17), which shows a more complete derivation of *John left*. (This time we will consider the movement of *John* to Spec TP, ignoring other functional categories.)

(17)
i.   Select John.
ii.   Select left.
iii. Merge(John, left) = {John, left}.
iv.   Select T.
v.   Merge(T, {John, left}) = {T, {John, left}}.
vi.   Copy John.
vii. Merge(John, {T, {John, left}}) = {John, {T, {John, left}}}.

In this derivation the interpretational properties of *left* are satisfied, since *left* takes *John* as an argument. In addition, the morphological properties of T are satisfied, since Case and EPP are checked against *John* in the Spec of TP before Spell-Out. The problem with this derivation is that there is an alternative, shown in (18).

(18)
i.   Select left.
ii.   Select T.
iii. Merge(T, left) = {T, left}.
iv.   Select John.
v.   Merge(John, {T, left}) = {John, {T, left}}.

This derivation satisfies the morphological properties of T (Case and EPP), but does not satisfy the interpretational properties of *left*. (On the assumption that *John* must be dominated by a projection of *left* in order to be interpreted as an argument, see (20) and (21).) In addition, note that (18) is significantly shorter than (17), since it involves no movement of *John*. If we adopted global economy (and the assumption that the reference set is determined by the Numeration), we would expect (18) to block (17). This is clearly undesirable, since the derivation in (18) is uninterpretable.[12] One way to solve this dilemma and maintain global economy is to adopt Chomsky's (1994) assumption that some economy conditions select the optimal derivation among the set of convergent derivations (e.g., Procrastinate). If the shorter derivation in (18) did not converge, it would not block the longer derivation in (17). One way of making (18) not converge is to assume that a violation of the θ-Criterion leads to nonconvergence. If this were true, (18) would be ruled out, since *left* does not assign a θ-role and *John* does not get a θ-role. This is, in fact, Chomsky's (1995: 315) analysis.

In order to evaluate this analysis, we must ask how plausible it is to assume that a violation of the θ-Criterion leads to nonconvergence. We cannot say that the verb has a θ-feature that must be checked off, and that the θ-feature is not checked off in (18). On this assumption, movement into a θ-position would be permitted; however, as we have seen, there is reason to think that such movement does not exist. Since most other cases of nonconvergence are limited to failure of one feature to check another, the hypothesis that derivation (18) does not converge is weakened.

Another reason to doubt the assumption that a violation of the θ-Criterion leads to nonconvergence is that the status of a θ-Criterion violation is not the same as the status of a nonconvergent derivation. Consider (19).

(19)
a. John seems that he is nice.
b. Arrived John.

Sentence (19a), in which all morphological features are appropriately checked, represents a violation of the θ-Criterion. In (19b), the Case feature of the finite T has not been checked, and there is no violation of the θ-Criterion (given that "arrive" is unaccusative). The question is whether there is a qualitative difference in unacceptability between these two sentences. It seems clear that there is, although many other examples should be checked. These sentences suggest that a violation of the θ-Criterion yields a violation that is qualitatively different from a nonconvergent derivation. In other words, there is no point to ranking the above violations as to which one is better or worse; they are just very different. This seems to suggest (in a very tentative way) that a violation of the θ-Criterion does not lead to nonconvergence, since otherwise the violations should be comparable in effect.

Therefore, we have two arguments against the hypothesis that a violation of the θ-Criterion leads to nonconvergence. But if we do not adopt this assumption, how can we ensure that the shorter derivation (18) does not block the longer derivation (17)? This question simply does not arise under local economy. All the operations of both derivations satisfy local economy. For example, step (17iii) is motivated, since the insertion of *John* is motivated by Integration. Therefore, both (17) and (18) are allowed by economy conditions (Minimality and Last Resort). The remaining question is why the derivation in (18) is blocked. One possibility I have already mentioned is that (18) simply yields an LF with no interpretation. In other words, if *John* is inserted in Spec T it cannot receive a θ-role, and so the structure is uninterpretable at LF. (I will return to this assumption in (20).)

The above discussion can be summarized as follows: It is possible to maintain global economy in the face of such derivations as (17) and (18) if it is assumed that a violation of the θ-Criterion leads to nonconvergence. On the other hand, there is little evidence for this assumption. The alternative is to adopt local economy, where no additional assumptions about convergence and the θ-Criterion are needed. Although (17) and (18) are equally economical (locally), (18) is uninterpretable.

Analyzing the derivation in (18) can shed further light on the nature of θ-role assignment. The question arises as to why the verb in (18) cannot raise at LF to T and then assign its θ-role to *John* in Spec TP. If this were possible, then the derivation in (18) should yield (after head movement at LF) an interpretable derivation. What we need is the condition shown in (20).

(20)
If X is adjoined to Y, X cannot assign a θ-role to Spec Y.

This prohibits V raising to T and assigning a θ-role to Spec T. If θ-role assignment were a form of feature checking, this would be possible (since feature checking involves the notion of a checking domain, defined in chapter 2).

Let us attempt to derive this generalization (which, to my knowledge, has not been previously noted): According to Hale and Keyser (1993), a DP is interpreted by virtue of its position in a structure. Let us suppose that these rules are of the form shown in (21).

(21)
The DP specifier of a VP whose complement is an AP/PP is interpreted as an individual that undergoes a change resulting in a state described by AP/PP.

There may be a number of simple rules of this type, accounting for the interpretation of external arguments, small clauses, and other essential syntactic configurations.[13] Now, given this rule of interpretation, consider again the derivation in (18). Note that the Spec of TP is in the checking domain of T, but the Spec of TP is not the Spec of VP. Therefore, no rule of interpretation concerning the VP could apply to Spec TP. In other words, assuming that a derivation such as (18) cannot take place, we have gained crucial evidence for a theory of θ-roles along the lines of Hale and Keyser 1993, where θ-roles are really the result of simple rules of interpretation applying to basic syntactic structures.

To review why Chomsky (1994: 429) states that a violation of the θ-Criterion leads to nonconvergence, consider (22) and (23).

(22)
a. There$_i$ seems [t$_i$ to be a man in the room].
b. *There seems [a man to be in the room].

(23)
a. *I$_i$ believe [t$_i$ to be a man in the room].
b. I believe [a man to be in the room].

According to Chomsky (1994: 428), the derivation leading to (22a) blocks the derivation leading to (22b). Chomsky wants to prevent the derivation leading to (23a) from blocking the derivation leading to (23b). In order to do this, he proposes that the derivation in (23a) is not convergent, since the chain (I, t) lacks a θ-role (movement to Spec *believe* being, according to Chomsky, excluded by Greed). (In this chapter I will not analyze the contrast between (22) and (23). I will analyze these structures in greater detail in chapter 5, where I will show that it is not necessary to assume that a violation of the θ-Criterion leads to nonconvergence to explain these sentences.)

I therefore conclude that there is no reason to suppose that a violation of the θ-Criterion leads to nonconvergence.

4.2.1 An Alternative

Watanabe (1995) proposes a modification of Integration. This modification is stated in (24).

(24) *Lexical Integration*
Every constituent must either
i. be dominated by another constituent, satisfying the lexical selectional property of the head of the dominating projection or
ii. dominate every other constituent (the root).

In other words, on Watanabe's proposal selectional properties drive Merge operations. Watanabe makes this proposal in the course of discussing properties of

causative constructions. He analyzes some causative constructions as involving a causative affix that selects an Agr_SP complement, and he analyzes other
causative constructions (Japanese) as involving a causative affix that selects a
TP complement. These selectional properties are checked at Merge, and in fact
they motivate the Merge operation.

Watanabe gives two reasons for preferring this approach over an approach
where the selectional properties of the causative affixes are checked at LF.
First, the distinction between Agr_SP and TP is lost at LF, if Agr_SP is rendered invisible when its N and V features are checked. Second, Watanabe raises the possibility that categorial features play no role at all at the LF interface, but rather
play a role only during the derivation (for example, the property that the Case
feature of DP is checked by T would not be stated at LF).

Evaluating Watanabe's proposal depends on the correctness of his analysis
of selection in causative constructions and on the correctness of his assumptions
about what information is available at LF. I will not attempt to evaluate either
of these factors; I will simply point out that even if we accept Watanabe's proposal there is still evidence that a selection-blind property of Integration exists.
Consider (25), in which the VP shown in (26) is constructed as an intermediate
representation (the DP is *the ball*, and the PP is *to Mary*).

(25)
John threw the ball to Mary.

(26)

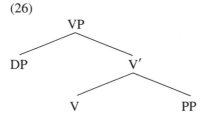

At the point where the DP *the ball* is merged with V′, we must ask what selectional properties are checked. If we adopt the view that θ-role assignment is
purely an interpretive process, restricted to the LF interface, θ-role assignment
cannot drive the Merge operation. Similarly, if the Case features of DP are checked
by LF movement of the DP (or alternatively, its Case features) to the checking
domain of some functional projection (see chapter 2 for discussion), then the
Case feature of DP cannot drive the Merge operation either (no Case checking
relation having been established by the Merge operation). In fact, at the point
in the derivation where the DP is merged with V′ there is no relation at all between the DP and the V′ except that they are sisters and they are both daugh-

ters of VP. Therefore, Watanabe's Integration condition is too strong for this case, but my Integration condition is just right.

I leave it to further research to eliminate altogether Watanabe's stronger form of Integration.

4.3 Binary Branching

One significant property of phrase structure appears to be that it is binary branching.[14] Chomsky (1993), following a suggestion by Akira Watanabe, proposes to derive this property of phrase structure from the binary nature of Generalized Transformations. He states that "the binarity of GT comes close to entailing that X-bar structures are restricted to binary branching." Chomsky (1994: 396) basically adopts this approach, except that in his revised account the binary nature of GT follows from the binary nature of Merge. In other words, Merge takes two elements α and β and combines them into the structure K={k, {α,β}}, where k is the label of K and {α,β} is the set of constituents of K.

In this section I will introduce a new version of Merge, called unrestricted Merge, that is simply a generalized grouping operation with no constraints on it. I will show that binary branching may be viewed as the result of Merge's being constrained by Minimality (local economy). Consider the definitions of Merge given in (27) and (28). (I will give more precise definitions shortly.)

(27) *Unrestricted Merge*
a. applies to zero, one, two or more constituents
b. applies to any constituents, whether or not they have already been merged before ("internal Merge").

(28) *Restricted Merge*
a. applies to exactly two constituents
b. applies only to constituents that have not already been merged (no "internal Merge").

Now consider (29) and (30), which show the structures that these two forms of Merge can form with the three constituents α, β, and γ.

(29) *Unrestricted Merge*
{α,β,γ}, {{α,β}, γ}, {α, {β,γ}}, {β, {α,γ}}, {{α}, {β}, {γ}}, {{ }, {α}, {β}, {γ}}, {{α,β}, {α,β,γ}}, {{α,β}, {β,γ}}, etc.

(30) *Restricted Merge*
{α, {β,γ}}, {β, {α,γ}}, {γ, {α,β}}

Clearly, unrestricted Merge generates many more possibilities than restricted Merge. If we are to adopt unrestricted Merge, we must show how most of the infinite possibilities are blocked.

We will see that it is possible to restrict the possible structures allowed by unrestricted Merge by appeal to very general principles, including economy of derivation. The basic idea is that phrase structure is binary because binary Merge is the smallest operation that will ensure that some structure actually gets built. In other words, binary branching will be seen to be a result of Minimality. If this idea can be worked out, adopting unrestricted Merge will allow us to perceive a deep relationship between movement and phrase structure: that both are subject to Minimality. As a unification of constraints on two different aspects of grammar (projection and movement), surely this counts as elegant.

As a start, let us put aside the possibility of internal merger (in other words, Merge that applies to constituents that have already been merged) until section 4.5. For now, let us concentrate on binary branching.

We can formalize these two possibilities a little more using as a starting point the definition in section 1.1 (see Chomsky 1995: 226). A derivation is a mapping from a Numeration N to LF (excluding the phonological component). A step in the derivation may be formalized as a set $\Sigma = \{SO_1, SO_2, \ldots, SO_n\}$ of syntactic objects. The set Σ is the set derived from the Numeration by successive applications of Select, Move, Merge, and Delete. At each point in the derivation, Merge takes a pair of syntactic objects (SO_i, SO_j) and replaces them in Σ by a new combined syntactic object: SO_k.

In other words, there are two components to Merge. First, Merge specifies a pair of syntactic objects, and forms a new syntactic object based on them. Second, it removes the original syntactic objects from the set Σ. There are obviously many ways of making this operation more precise. For example, let us define restricted Merge as in (31).

(31)
Given a set $\Sigma = \{SO_1, SO_2, \ldots, SO_n\}$ and a subset Σ' (consisting of exactly two elements) of Σ, then Merge(Σ') is defined as the following complex operation:
i.   make Σ' as a member of Σ (recall a constituent is just a set of constituents)
ii. define Head(Σ') = Head(SO) for some SO in Σ' (SO = syntactic object)
iii. remove the elements of Σ' from Σ.

Let us see how this definition works. Consider the subset $\Sigma' = \{\alpha, \beta\}$ of the set $\Sigma = \{\alpha, \beta, \gamma\}$. Merge($\Sigma'$) is defined as follows: First, we add $\{\alpha, \beta\}$ to the set Σ, forming the set $\{\alpha, \beta, \gamma, \{\alpha, \beta\}\}$. Second, we define the head of $\{\alpha, \beta\}$ as

Head($\{\alpha,\beta\}$) = Head(α) (see (3) above). Third, we remove the elements of Σ' = $\{\alpha, \beta\}$ from the newly modified $\Sigma = \{\alpha, \beta, \gamma, \{\alpha, \beta\}\}$. This yields the set $\Sigma = \{\gamma, \{\alpha, \beta\}\}$.[15]

Still putting aside the issue of internal Merge, we can define unrestricted Merge by simply removing "consisting of exactly two elements" from the above definition, thereby allowing any subset Σ' (regardless of cardinality) of Σ to be the argument of Merge.

Given these preliminary considerations, consider the constituents α, β, and γ. Consider the ways in which these constituents can be combined by unrestricted Merge. Two possibilities are given in (32) and (33).

(32)

i. Merge(α,β,γ) = $\{\alpha,\beta,\gamma\}$.

(33)

i. Merge(α,β) = $\{\alpha,\beta\}$.

ii. Merge($\gamma, \{\alpha,\beta\}$) = $\{\gamma \{\alpha,\beta\}\}$.

The derivation in (32) is blocked, since it violates Minimality. At the point in the derivation where the operation Merge(α,β,γ) is possible, the operation Merge(α,β) (which involves the merging of fewer elements) is also possible. Therefore, we can derive binary branching from Minimality and unrestricted Merge.

In order for this analysis to be made rigorous, we must redefine Minimality. Recall that in section 2.4 Minimality was defined as in (34).

(34)

α can raise to a target K only if there is no operation (satisfying Last Resort) Move β targeting K, where β is closer to K.

This definition makes reference to Move, which is not involved here. Consider the more general formulation (35).

(35)

An operation OP (satisfying Last Resort) may apply only if there no smaller operation OP' (satisfying Last Resort).

The crucial undefined notion is that of *smaller* operation. In order for one operation OP to be smaller than another operation OP', there must be some way of comparing the operations. I will assume that any possible way to compare operations along some dimension comes into play in evaluating Minimality. In the case of Move, Minimality chooses the operation that has the shortest path of movement (in the sense of (34)). In the case of Merge, Minimality chose the operation that combines the smallest number of elements.

This may seem like an unsatisfactory explanation of binary branching in terms of Minimality, simply because what is minimized in each case is so different. I view this as one aspect of the computational system. The computational system looks at an operation and compares it to any operation with which it can be compared along some dimension (shortest path, least number of elements, and possibly other dimensions). In this sense the definition of Minimality in (35) is completely general.[16]

In a sense, derivation (32) is shorter than derivation (33), since (32) involves one step and (33) involves two steps. Therefore, if we were to adopt the Shortest Derivation Requirement of chapter 1, we might expect the derivation in (32) to block (33) (assuming that two derivations that start from the same Numeration are in the same reference set for selecting the optimal derivation).

Consider the above account in light of the notion that economy conditions select the optimal derivations from among the set of convergent derivations (a global notion, as discussed in chapter 1). If we adopt this way of defining economy conditions, it may be possible for three constituents to be merged, if not doing so would result in a nonconvergent derivation. For example, a VP could have the form {V, DP, DP} if otherwise the Case of some DP would not be checked. This possibility does not seem attested. In this respect, ternary branching is unlike Procrastinate (on Chomsky's (1994) analysis), where X can move before Spell-Out (which is more costly than LF movement), if covert movement would result in a nonconvergent derivation. Since such cases of ternary branching do not seem to be attested, this counts as (very weak) evidence in favor of the idea that economy conditions are inviolable (see chapter 1).

In the above discussion, I have reduced binary branching to a case of Minimality. Earlier in the chapter, I showed how Merge was subject to Last resort. Therefore, Merge and Move are perfectly parallel in being subject to local economy.[17]

The fact that properties of phrase structures can be recast as results of the economy conditions strikes me as a deep unification of the properties of the grammar.

4.4   Non-Branching Projection

Having shown that binary branching reduces to economy of derivation, I will now discuss the ban on non-branching projection (see Chomsky 1994: 398). In a theory where there are no non-branching projections, structures such as (36) (where there are three non-branching projections: first, the node D is a projection of *the*; second, the node N′ is a projection of *man*; third the node NP is a projection of N′) are ruled out. Chomsky (1994) suggests that a representation such as (37) would be more appropriate. In fact, the most precise representation is the one formed from sets, the representation shown here as (37) being a convenient representational device.

(36)

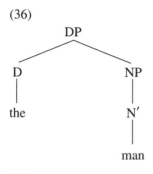

(37)

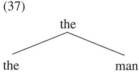

For Chomsky (1994), this result follows from the fact that Merge is a binary operation, combining two constituents α and β to form a third:

(38)
Merge(α, β) = γ.

Since we are assuming unrestricted Merge, which can take any set Σ of structures as an argument, the operations (39) and (40) are possible.

(39)
Merge(α) = {α}

(40)
Merge(α, { }) = {α, { }}

It seems reasonable that the result of either of these derivations is what is called empirically a non-branching projection.[18] In the case of (39), the result is different from α, but has the same head. In (40), there has been a merger with the empty set.

I will suggest that (40) is ruled out by economy. The operation (39) is ruled out in a somewhat different way. I will argue that there can be no unary merger in grammar on the basis of conceptual necessity.

To be concrete about the issues involved, consider three derivations of *John laughed*: one in which *laugh* has as its object an abstract cognate object and two in which *laugh* does not have such an object. I will show that the derivations that do not involve cognate objects can be excluded for principled reasons.

Consider (41)–(43).

(41)

i.   Select laugh.

ii. Select LAUGH (abstract cognate object).

iii. Merge(laugh, LAUGH) = {laugh, LAUGH}.

iv. Select John.

v.   Merge(John, {laugh, LAUGH}) = {John, {laugh, LAUGH}}.

(42)

i.   Select laugh.

ii. Merge(laugh, { }) = {laugh, { }}.

iii. Select John.

iv. Merge(John, {laugh, { }}) = {John, {laugh, { }}}.

(43)

i.   Select laugh.

ii. Merge(laugh)= {laugh}.

iii. Select John.

iv. Merge(John, {laugh}) = {John, {laugh}}.

Derivation (41) is what Hale and Keyser (1993) proposed for the structure of unergative verbs. Derivation (42) involves a non-branching projection of *laugh* putting *John* into the specifier of the projection headed by *laugh* (see (42iii) and (42iv)).

In order to obtain the empty set in (42ii), it would be necessary to perform Merge() = { }. But this operation does not satisfy Last Resort, since it does not satisfy the properties of any element. In particular, it does not satisfy Integration, since no constituent is affected by Merge. Thus, the step (42ii) could never have taken place. This argument has the strong consequence that there is no empty category devoid of features. In other words, at LF, there can never be any empty expletive.

Ruling out derivation (43) is a little more difficult. Step (43ii) does not satisfy any morphological properties of *laugh*, but it does satisfy the Integration property of *laugh*, since *laugh* is integrated in a larger phrase. Thus, although the derivation (43) seems to satisfy Last Resort (because the Integration property is satisfied), it must be ruled out.

I have already noted that Merge{α,β,γ} is more costly than Merge{α,β}, and that this fact yields the binary nature of phrase structure by Minimality. Given this conclusion, it is reasonable to assume that the least costly operation at any step in the derivation will be to merge individual constituents. If that is so, the continuation of (43ii) will be (43′).

(43′)
i.   Select laugh.
ii. Merge(laugh)= {laugh}.
iii. Merge({laugh}) = {{laugh}}.
iv. Merge({{laugh}}) = {{{laugh}}}.
v.   Continue indefinitely.

In fact, it should never be possible for any derivation to combine two elements, since merging a single element is the least costly operation. As a consequence, every utterance should consist of a single word (although that word may be arbitrarily deeply embedded). This is unacceptable, since one of the basic facts about language is that it allows for sentences.

Therefore, we must stipulate that Merge has as a requirement that the set Σ' it takes as an argument has two or more elements. This kind of stipulation, since it follows from the most basic considerations about the empirical adequacy of the theory and since it must be made universally, seems to be a rather minimal departure from a system with no assumptions at all about the form of Merge.

4.5   The Strict Cycle

One derivation I have not so far dealt with is shown in (44).

(44)
i. Merge(α,β) = {α,β}
ii. Merge(γ, α) = {γ,α}

This derivation poses the question why it is not possible to go back and merge α with γ. This Merge operation could form either an adjunction structure or a non-adjunction structure; both cases must be blocked. Intuitively, this derivation violates the strict cycle (or, in the framework of Chomsky 1993, the "extension condition"). In a truly minimalist framework, we would not like to appeal to the strict cycle, or the extension condition; rather, we would like to derive their effects from more basic assumptions.[19]

Another way of blocking the derivation (44) is to appeal to the definition of (unrestricted) Merge, repeated here as (45).

(45)

Given a set $\Sigma = \{SO_1, SO_2, \ldots, SO_n\}$ and a subset Σ' of Σ, then Merge(Σ') is defined as the following operation:

i.   make Σ' as a member of Σ

ii. define Head(Σ') = Head(SO) for some SO in Σ' (SO = syntactic object)

iii. remove the elements of Σ' from Σ.

This definition would not allow the derivation in (44), since Σ is modified by recursive applications of Merge, each time removing the merged elements from Σ. Consider in detail step (44i), paying attention to the contents of Σ.

(46)

a. $\Sigma = \{\alpha, \beta, \gamma\}$

b. Merge(α, β) = $\{\alpha, \beta\}$

   $\Sigma = \{\gamma, \{\alpha, \beta\}\}$

If we start the computation with the Σ in (46a), the operation Merge(α,β) not only adds a new element to Σ but also removes α and β from Σ. Since the elements that are merged must, according to (45), be elements of Σ, it follows that (44ii) will never be permitted.

However, there is no conceptual reason why the elements that may be merged must come from the set Σ in (45). There is one other easily definable set from which the elements that are merged could be drawn. This set includes, intuitively, any constituent that has been formed in the derivation.[20] Consider the definition (47).

(47)

Given a set $\Sigma = \{SO_1, SO_2, \ldots, SO_n\}$ and a set T every member of which is a member of Σ or a constituent dominated by a member of Σ, Merge(T) is defined as the following operation:

i.   make T as a member of Σ

ii. define Head(T) = Head(SO) for some SO in T (SO = syntactic object)

iii. remove the elements of T from Σ.

Under this definition, any set of constituents whatsoever may be merged, including constituents from the set Σ and any subconstituent of any structure so far formed. In a way, this is the most unrestrictive (and perhaps, in one sense, the simplest) version of Merge, since it allows Merge to operate on any set of constituents whatsoever.

Now consider again the derivation (44), repeated and expanded in (48).

(48)
a. $\Sigma = \{\alpha, \beta, \gamma\}$
b. Merge(α, β) = $\{\alpha, \beta\}$
   $\Sigma = \{\gamma, \{\alpha, \beta\}\}$
c. Merge(γ, α) = $\{\gamma, \alpha\}$
   $\Sigma = \{\{\gamma, \alpha\}, \{\alpha, \beta\}\}$

The last step in (48c) is in accordance with the definition of Merge in (47), since γ is in Σ in (48b), and α is a dominated by $\{\alpha, \beta\}$ a member of Σ. We have now eliminated the extension condition, the strict cycle, and the definition of Merge as possible ways to block this derivation. Fortunately, there is a very plausible way to block this derivation in terms of conditions needed for completely independent reasons. It can be shown that the resulting structure violates Kayne's (1994) Linear Correspondence Axiom.

Consider the structure illustrated in (49).

(49)

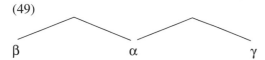

β α γ

In this representation, neither β nor γ c-commands the other, and therefore neither β nor γ asymmetrically c-commands the other. Therefore, the terminals of β and γ (or β and γ themselves, if they are terminals) will not be ordered. Therefore, the assigned ordering will not be total, and the LCA will be violated.

In order to see our system work with a concrete example, consider (50)—a case of countercyclic merger, where *John* is inserted into Spec VP countercyclically.

(50)
i.   Select saw
     $\Sigma = \{saw\}$
ii. Select me
     $\Sigma = \{saw, me\}$
iii. Merge(saw, me) = $\{saw, me\}$
     $\Sigma = \{\{saw, me\}\}$
iv. Select T
     $\Sigma = \{T, \{saw, me\}\}$
v.   Merge(T, $\{saw, me\}$)
     $\Sigma = \{\{T, \{saw, me\}\}\}$
vi. Select John
     $\Sigma = \{John, \{T, \{saw, me\}\}\}$
vii. Merge(John, $\{saw, me\}$) = $\{John, \{saw, me\}\}$
     $\Sigma = \{\{T, \{saw, me\}\}, \{John, \{saw, me\}\}\}$.[21]

In this derivation, *John* is inserted countercyclically into Spec VP. Note that after *John* is merged with {*saw, me*}, it is not c-commanded by T. This is true, since there is a constituent dominating T (that is TP) that does not dominate *John*. Therefore, the set of ordered pairs in d(A) is the following: ⟨T, saw⟩, ⟨T, me⟩, ⟨John, saw⟩, ⟨John, me⟩. Because there is no ordering relationship established between T and *John*, this representation is excluded by the LCA. Note also that there is no linear relationship established between the verb *saw* and its complement *me*. Since Chomsky (1994: 417) treats this case, I will not discuss it.

We could avoid the above problem with the LCA if, after merging *John* with {*saw, me*} in (50vii), we replaced (or redefined) the complement of T, which is {*saw, me*}, with the constituent {*John*, {*saw, me*}}. Chomsky (1994: 402) assumes that this kind of replacement operation exists, at least in the case of covert movement (to which I will return shortly). However, such a replacement operation would greatly complicate Merge, and so it is to be avoided. A provision would have to be added to the effect that if Merge(α,β) = γ, where α is embedded in another constituent, α must be replaced by γ. Since this provision complicates the definition of Merge and prevents us from accounting for the cycle in terms of the independently needed LCA, there is no reason to believe that replacement is possible.

Empirically, prohibiting countercyclic merger is important. If countercyclic merger were possible, it would be possible to generate sentences like (51).

(51)
*John Mary saw.
"Mary saw John."

Under the Agr_S theory, in this sentence the complement of the verb *John* would raise to Spec Agr_SP before *Mary* was inserted into Spec VP. Since *Mary* is not present, raising of *John* would incur no violation of Minimality. At LF, *Mary* would raise to Spec Agr_O to check the accusative Case of the verb.

My account of the strict cycle carries over straightforwardly to Move. Consider (52) and the two possible derivations shown in (53) and (54).[22]

(52)
a. [$_{VP}$ was stolen [a picture of who]]
b. *who$_i$ was a picture of t$_i$ stolen

(53)
a. [a picture of who] moves to Spec Agr_S
b. *who* moves to Spec CP

(54)

a. *who* moves to Spec CP

b. [a picture of t] moves to Spec Agr$_S$

The representation in (52a) is a point in the derivation of (52b). The derivation in (53) is the cyclic derivation. In this derivation the movement of *who* violates the CED. The derivation in (54) is the countercyclic derivation, the movement of [a picture of t] violates the strict cycle.

On the theory outlined above, when [a picture of t] moves to Spec Agr$_S$ in the countercyclic derivation, a phrase structure will be created that violates the LCA. This is so, since the terminals of [a picture of t] will be unordered with respect to *who* in Spec CP.

As was pointed out in chapter 1, Chomsky (1994: 412) suggests that the countercyclic derivation of (54) can be blocked by economy of derivation. I reiterate Chomsky's explanation here. In (54), the movement of *who* is longer (in terms of the number of XPs traversed) than in (53). In (53), *who* crosses the following nodes: {PP, NP, DP, Agr$_S$P}. In (47), *who* crosses the following nodes: {PP, NP, DP, VP, AuxP, TP, Agr$_S$P}.[23] Therefore, the movement path of *who* is longer in (54) than in (53).

The problem with this account is that it relies on global economy. Note that the movement of *who* to Spec CP in (54a) is blocked not because there is a shorter possible movement of *who* at that step in the derivation, but rather because at a different step in the derivation (53b) there is a shorter movement of *who*. Therefore, my account of the strict-cycle effects in terms of the LCA avoids postulating global economy for this case.[24]

Finally, consider another example where our approach blocks countercyclic movement. Consider Icelandic, a language in which there is overt object shift. Assume for the sake of discussion that a shifted object moves into Spec Agr$_O$.[25] Now consider the derivations (55) and (56), where VP = {V, DP}.

(55)

i.   Select Agr$_O$

ii. Merge(Agr$_O$, VP) = {Agr$_O$, VP}

iii. Copy DP

iv. Merge(DP, {Agr$_O$, VP}) = {DP, {Agr$_O$, VP}}

v.   Select T

vi. Merge(T, {DP, {Agr$_O$, VP}}) = {T, {DP, {Agr$_O$, VP}}}

(56)
i.   Select Agr_O
ii. Merge(Agr_O, VP) = {Agr_O, VP}
iii. Select T
iv. Merge(T, {Agr_O, VP}) = {T, {Agr_O, VP}}
v.   Copy DP
vi. Merge(DP, {Agr_O, VP}) = {DP, {Agr_O, VP}}

The derivation in (55) proceeds cyclically; the derivation in (56) does not. In (56), the terminals of DP and T are unordered with respect to each other, and so the derivation violates the LCA.

One problem with the above account is that covert object shift seems to be countercyclic. In fact, this was the one reason that Chomsky (1994: 402) postulated that replacement (or redefinition) of terms was possible. I will address the issue of covert object shift below. Since I have explicitly rejected the notion of replacement (or redefinition) of terms, an alternative to Chomsky's analysis will be necessary.

4.5.1 Head Movement
It is clear that head movement is always countercyclic. Consider the derivation in (57), which involves V movement to T. (The verb is an unaccusative verb, for which the object raises to Spec TP.)

(57)
a. Select V
b. [build DP]
c. Merge(V, DP) = {V, DP}
d. Select T
e. Merge(T, {V, DP}) = {T, {V, DP}}
f. Copy V
g. Merge(T , V) = {V, $\langle$T, T$\rangle$}
h. Copy DP
i. Merge(DP, {T, {V, DP}}) = {DP, {T, {V, DP}}}

Now consider the asymmetric c-command relations in this sentence. The subject DP asymmetrically c-commands T, and T asymmetrically c-commands the lower copy of V and the lower copy of DP. The problem is that the subject DP does not c-command the upper copy of V, since the complex {V, $\langle$T, T$\rangle$} is not dominated by any projection that dominates the subject DP. Similarly, the upper copy of V does not c-command the subject DP. Therefore, there is no c-command relation at all between these elements, and they will be unordered with respect to one another, violating the LCA.

There are conceivable ways of rescuing the derivation (57). For example, it could be suggested that the reason why head movement can violate LCA is because of the special nature of Morphology. Chomsky (1994: 394) proposes there exists a component Morphology that "constructs word-like units that are then subjected to further processes." This seems reasonable, as there are many aspects of morphology that we would not like to attribute to either the syntax or the phonological components (for example, the Spell-Out rules of inflectional morphology). I have postulated that LCA operates after Spell-Out. I can be more precise and postulate that LCA applies after Morphology. On these assumptions, the condition (58) would save the derivation in (57).

(58)
Morphology renders a head adjunction structure invisible to the LCA.

Under this condition, head adjunction is never a problem for the LCA.[26]

However, there is another problematic aspect to the derivation in (57). The upper copy of the verb does not c-command the verbal trace (the lower copy of the verb). There is no segment or category that dominates the upper copy of the verb and also dominates the trace. If c-command requires that at least some segment or category of an antecedent dominate its trace, then the verb does not c-command its trace in (57). This seems undesirable, since in most (perhaps all) other cases of movement an antecedent c-commands its trace. If this problem is significant, it necessitates rethinking the whole formalism of adjunction and in particular how adjunction interacts with head movement.[27]

One promising approach is that of Bobaljik (1995), who allows the equivalent of head movement across phrase markers. How would this work in our system? Consider (57′) as an alternative to the derivation presented in (57).

(57′)
a. Select V
b. [build DP]
c. Merge(V, DP) = {V, DP}
d. Select T
e. Copy V
f. Merge(V, T) = {V, ⟨T, T⟩}
g. Merge({V, ⟨T,T⟩}, {V, DP}) = {{V, ⟨T,T⟩}, {V, DP}}
h. Copy DP
i. Merge(DP, {{V, ⟨T,T⟩}, {V, DP}}) = {DP, {{V, ⟨T,T⟩}, {V, DP}}}

Steps (57′e) and (57′f) amount to movement of the verb across phrase markers. Note that the output of this derivation does not violate the LCA (as can be readily verified). In particular, note that in this example the subject DP asymmetrically c-commands the upper copy of the verb, since TP dominates the DP and also dominates the upper copy of the verb. In addition, the verb adjoined to T does c-command its trace, since only one segment of T dominates the V. I leave this approach as a very promising line to develop.

4.5.2 LF Movement

The one particular feature of LF movement is that it is always countercyclic. This can be illustrated in the Agr_O framework with a case of LF object shift:

(59)
i. $\{T, \{Agr_O, VP\}\}$ (pre-Spell-Out structure)
ii. Copy DP (at LF)
iii. $Merge(DP, \{Agr_O, \{V, DP\}\}) = \{DP, \{Agr_O, \{V, DP\}\}\}$

It is easy to see that this derivation would violate the LCA if the LCA held at LF. However, we have explicitly adopted the assumption that the LCA holds only after Spell-Out. Therefore, LF movement never causes a violation of the LCA, and it is allowed to be countercyclic.

Chomsky (1995: 272) suggests that LF movement is always movement of features and never movement of full phrasal categories. For example, LF object shift of a DP should be analyzed as the movement of the formal features of the DP (Case, D, ϕ-features) to adjoin to the head that will check these features. This type of movement, since it occurs at LF, would never violate the LCA either (the LCA being restricted to following Spell-Out).

The result that LF movement may be countercyclic runs counter to many empirical studies that deal with transitivity constraints on certain constructions (expletive constructions, stylistic inversion in French, quotative inversion in English, *ga-no* conversion in Japanese). These studies include Bures 1993, Jonas and Bobaljik 1993, Branigan and Collins 1993, and Watanabe 1994. However, as we saw in chapter 2, at least for the case of quotative inversion, no LF cycle is needed.[28]

So far we have seen how LF movement does not pose a problem for the LCA, since the LCA applies after Spell-Out. In view of this, LF movement may appear to be countercyclic. But there is another possible analysis: We could deny that there is LF movement. Bobaljik (1995) suggests such an approach in passing. He suggests that all movement is overt in the sense that syntactic computations produce a single output that is then fed to the semantic interpretive (LF) and morpho-phonological (PF) components of the grammar. The apparent effects of covert vs. overt movement may be related to which part of chain is deleted. If the head is deleted, we have the appearance of covert movement. If the tail is deleted, we have the appearance of overt movement. A very similar approach, without derivations altogether, is developed by Brody (1995).

Though I find such an approach suggestive, there are certain differences between LF movement and overt movement that collapsing the two would fail to capture. Consider the examples in (60). (This analysis is from Collins 1993.)

(60)
a. *[John to be nice], I considered
b. *How likely to be a storm was there
c. . . . and go the store, John *(did)

The unacceptability of all three of these examples may be explained by the following principle:

(61)
Suppose α contains a constituent β and α undergoes overt movement. Then β may not undergo covert movement to a position outside of α.

In other words, overt movement bleeds covert movement. In (60a), *John* will not be able to raise to its Case position (perhaps Spec Agr_O) at LF, since the embedded TP has been fronted. In (60b), *a storm* will not be able to adjoin to *there*, since the AP has been fronted. In (60c), the verb *go* will not be able to raise and check the V feature of T, so *do*-support is necessary. There are alternative accounts of the data in (60), but none with the generality of the LF movement analysis just given.

No condition such as (61) holds for overt movement. In other words, as (62) shows, overt movement does not seem to bleed overt movement.[29]

(62)
a. ?How likely to arrive on time was John
b. . . . and arrested by the police, John was

In (62a), *John* is raised from infinitival TP to the matrix Spec TP position before movement of the AP to Spec CP. In (62b), movement of *John* (as part of passivization) precedes topicalization of the VP.

4.6 Numeration

Throughout the book, we have been assuming Chomsky's (1994, 1995) characterization of a derivation as a mapping from a Numeration to LF (branching at Spell-Out to PF). In this model a Numeration is formed before the derivation begins. The Numeration is defined as a set of pairs (LI, i), where LI is a lexical item and i is the index that tells how many times LI is to be selected from the Numeration. An element LI in the Numeration is selected (the operation Select) from the Numeration, reducing its index by one. After that, one of the possible syntactic operations (Select, Merge, Move, Delete) applies.

The presence of a Numeration in the theory of grammar is not necessary in the same way that the lexicon and the PF and LF interfaces are necessary. The Numeration is a purely grammar internal structure that is observed only through its (sometimes subtle) consequences for the observable structures generated by the grammar. In this sense, postulating a Numeration is a clear departure from minimalist assumptions, unless it can be shown that there is strong empirical evidence for it.

In this section, I will propose an alternative characterization of the derivation that does not use a Numeration. I will consider the evidence for the Numeration and show that it is weak. In chapter 5, I will return to the Numeration and show that it is not needed to explain certain derivations.

The lexicon is a set of lexical items. There must be some relation between the lexicon and the syntactic computation. Since the lexicon must be accessed for many different derivations, it is plausible that a derivation does not manipulate lexical items in the lexicon but rather manipulates *copies of* these elements. Therefore, the first step in any derivation will be to copy some lexical item out of the lexicon for grammatical operations to apply to. In this light, consider the derivation of the verb phrase *John see Mary*:

(63)
i.   Copy Mary (out of lexicon)
ii. Copy see (out of lexicon)
iii. Merge(see, Mary) = {see, Mary}
iv. Copy John(out of lexicon)
v.   Merge(John, {see, Mary}) = {John, {see, Mary}}

On this point of view there is no Numeration; there is simply a lexicon. There is no operation of Select either, since Select was an operation particular to the Numeration. (Select was a complex operation, reducing the indices of the elements of the Numeration.) Nor are their any reasons why lexical items should bear indices, as they did in the Numeration.[30]

There is a strong conceptual reason to adopt this simple approach. Note that on this approach "lexical insertion" involves a Copy operation and a Merge operation. These are exactly the same two operations that are involved in Move (= Copy + Merge). On this view "lexical insertion" is a kind of movement out of the lexicon. An example of movement as Copy and Merge is given in (64).

(64)
i.   {T, {V, DP}}
ii.   Copy DP
iii. Merge(DP, {T, {V, DP}}) = {DP, {T, {V, DP}}}

We can consider this from another point of view. Suppose that we assume that lexical insertion is done as specified above, using Copy and Merge. Then movement becomes an automatic possibility, since it involves no new operations. Looked at in this way, any grammar that allows lexical insertion will also allow movement. It would complicate the grammar greatly to block movement from occurring.

However, there are two differences between "lexicon insertion" and movement. First, we have postulated that lexical insertion (and more generally, Merge) is driven by the Integration property. This accounts for the fact that lexical insertion does not have to be accompanied by feature checking. On the other hand, movement is not driven by Integration. If it could be, we would expect movement to occur to any position, not just to positions of feature checking. How can we retain the parallel between lexical insertion and movement, pointed out above, while accounting for this fundamental difference?

I would like to suggest that the way to answer this problem is by considering the relationship between Copy and Merge in general. It seems to be the case that whenever Copy is used it is followed immediately by Merge. In the case of lexical insertion, an element is copied out of the lexicon and then merged into the structure. In the case of movement, an element is copied out of the tree and merged into another place in the tree. Therefore, let us assume that Copy and Merge together form a complex operation, and that it is this operation that must meet Last Resort.

In the case of pure merger of two already formed constituents, there is no Copy operation, and the Merge operation is driven by Integration. In the case of lexical insertion, a lexical item is not part of the tree, and so Integration motivates the Copy + Merge operation. In the case of movement, the element to be moved is already part of the structure,[31] so that movement (Copy + Merge) cannot satisfy Integration. The only alternative is feature checking.

The other difference between lexical insertion and movement is that movement results in the formation of a chain. This chain is needed for interpretation purposes at LF, each θ-role being assigned to a chain. On the other hand, lexicon insertion does not (in any obvious way) result in the formation of a chain. Without analyzing this difference in too much detail, it seems to be that the primary difference between lexical insertion and movement is that in the case of lexical insertion it is not possible to delete a lexical item after it has been copied. Such deletion would result in a smaller lexicon after each derivation, clearly the wrong prediction. Movement does not have this constraint. Suppose that a constituent XP has undergone Copy + Merge as the result of movement. There is no problem with deleting part of one of the copies (up to Recoverability). This deletion process gives rise to the fact that the lower copy of the chain is not overt at Spell-Out, and it may give rise to certain reconstruction effects at LF (Chomsky 1993).

Let us assume that a chain between XP and XP′ can be formed if deletion of one or part of either XP is possible. Then no chain would be possible in the case of lexical insertion. Although this is speculative, the relationship between deletion and chain formation seems a promising line to follow.

Now consider now Chomsky's (1994, 1995) reasons for postulating a Numeration.

First, the LF and PF representations must be compatible. That is, the LF and the PF associated with a particular derivation must be based on the same lexical choices (Chomsky 1995: 225). The notion of Numeration formalizes this requirement. I agree with Chomsky that it is a necessary feature of grammar that the LF and PF associated with a derivation must be based on the same lexical choices. On the other hand, it seems to me that this follows without the notion of Numeration. Any lexical item that is copied and merged into the derivation before Spell-Out will appear in both the LF and the PF representation (unless it is deleted as part of a chain). For lexical items that have a semantic, formal and phonological component LI = {S, F, P}, insertion will always have to happen before Spell-Out. Suppose, following Chomsky (1994, 1995: 229), that Spell-Out is the mechanism by which semantic features are stripped off before the derivation continues on to PF, and phonological features are stripped off before the derivation continues on to LF. If a lexical item of the form LI = {S, F, P} is inserted after Spell-Out in the derivation to LF, it will crash, for the simple reason that the phonological features will be uninterpretable at LF. Similarly, if a lexical item of the form LI = {S, F, P} is inserted after Spell-Out in the derivation to PF, it will crash. Only two cases remain: a semantically vacuous element could be inserted in the PF branch of the derivation (after Spell-Out), and a phonologically vacuous element could be inserted in the LF branch of the derivation. While it would be difficult to detect such cases, there is no good reason to doubt that they exist.[32]

Second, the Numeration fixes the reference set for determining optimal derivations. In other words, in order to decide whether derivation D is more economical that D', we only compare derivations that are based on the same Numeration. In a theory based on local economy there is less of a need for the Numeration.[33] Let me repeat the definition of economy:

(65)
Given a set of syntactic objects Σ which is part of derivation D, the decision about whether or not an operation OP may apply to Σ (as part of an optimal derivation) is made only on the basis of information available in Σ.

If this definition turns out to be empirically and conceptually adequate, there is no need to compare whole derivations. Therefore, if one of the functions of a Numeration is to determine the reference set of derivations that are compared, there is no need to have the Numeration. Rather, possible operations at a particular step in the derivation are being compared. For example, suppose that we have reached a step in a derivation where we have the set Σ of representations (a set of syntactic objects). At this point, we can do a movement operation, or Merge several of the objects, or Copy something out of the lexicon. Any operation that satisfies Minimality and Last Resort is permissible. There is no reference at all to a Numeration.[34]

There is one detail to be clarified in the system outlined above. Chomsky (1995: 236) assumes that optional features of a lexical item (for example, the accusative Case feature of a noun) are added to the lexical item when the Numeration is formed. Then the Numeration contains lexical items with a specification of optional features. In my system, there are two possibilities. First, these optional features could be available in the lexicon (i.e., each lexical item in the lexicon would be accompanied by a list of alternative forms based on the optional features). Second, the optional features could be added to the copy of the lexical item, before the item is merged. I see no way to decide between these options. Given these arguments against having a Numeration, and given the alternative advanced above, I reject Numeration as a valid construct.

There is one empirical domain in which Numeration has proved useful: in the discussion of the paradigm shown here as (66).

(66)
a. There seems to be someone in the room.
b. *There seems someone to be in the room.

Chomsky (1995: 344) makes crucial use of the Numeration. Since I am claiming that this notion may be eliminated, I will come back to this contrast in chapter 5 and give it a treatment based purely on local economy without a Numeration.

4.7   Conclusion

In this chapter I have shown how the economy conditions of Last Resort and Minimality apply to the building of constituent structure. Lexical Insertion and Merge are driven by a property called Integration. Binary branching is the consequence of Minimality's applying to Merge. In both cases the economy conditions are strictly local.

I have also shown how the strict cycle follows from Kayne's (1994) LCA. This is a welcome result, since there have been at least two treatments of strict-cycle effects in terms of global economy: Chomsky 1994 (p. 412) and Kitahara 1995.

Finally, I have shown how adopting local economy makes it possible to eliminate the concept of Numeration.

The resulting system is remarkably simple. Economy conditions (perhaps limited to Last Resort and Minimality) apply to all operations and are extremely easy to verify, having the properties of locality, independence, and inviolability. Movement is simply Copy followed by Merge, and lexical insertion is the same. Extra conditions and constructs do not exist. (There is no Numeration or strict-cycle condition.)

These results, made possible in large part by the adoption of local economy, seem to take us further down the path toward a strictly minimalist theory of syntactic derivations.

Chapter 5

Last Resort

This chapter takes as its starting point the intuition that syntactic operations must be motivated in some way; they do not occur for free. This is a form of economy: an operation occurs only if it is motivated. In this chapter, I will show how this fundamental assumption about syntactic operations plays a role in ECM constructions, in successive cyclic movement, and in the analysis of improper movement.

In chapter 1, I briefly characterized the definition of Greed in Chomsky 1994 as a global economy definition. In chapter 2, I gave a formalization of a local condition Last Resort, which I used in the analysis of locative and quotative inversion. In chapter 4, I extended the definition of Last Resort to apply to lexical insertion and pure Merge. In this chapter, I provide the motivation for the definition of Last Resort that was given in chapter 2. I repeat this definition here as (1).

(1)
Move raises α to the checking domain of a head H with a feature F only if the feature F of H enters into a checking relation with a feature F of α.

This definition relies on the notion of checking relation, given in (2).

(2)
F1 and F2 enter a checking relation iff F2 is in the checking domain of F1 and F1 is deleted. (F2 may also be deleted.)

I will concentrate here on implications of the definition of Last Resort for movement, to the exclusion of lexical insertion and pure Merge.

In section 5.1, I will give an overview of the problems inherent in Chomsky 1994 and in Chomsky and Lasnik 1993. In section 5.2, I will introduce the notion of asymmetric feature checking and show how Last Resort may be redefined on the basis of this definition. I will also review Chomsky's (1995) system of interpretable features, and show how it puts the notion of asymmetric feature checking on firmer ground. In section 5.3, I will discuss A′-movement in the context of Last Resort. In section 5.4, I will show how the definition of Last Resort allows me to dispense with the operation Form Chain. In section 5.5, I will show how the ban on improper movement follows from Last Resort.

5.1   Greed and Local Economy

One of the major economy conditions that Chomsky (1993; 1994: 14) has proposed is *Greed*:

(3)
Move α raises to a position β only if morphological properties of α itself would not otherwise be satisfied in the derivation.

This formulation is in fact closely related to the formulation of Chomsky and Lasnik (1993: 564): "Turning now to the last resort principle, its intuitive content was that operations should be permissible only if they form legitimate LF objects. We now relax that requirement, taking an operation to be permissible if it is a prerequisite to the formation of a legitimate LF object."

   Compare (3) to the stronger condition (4), which I will call for convenience *Greediest*.

(4)
Move α raises to a position β only if some morphological property of α itself is satisfied in position β.

In principle, Greediest is much stronger than Greed, as Greed allows an operation to take place if eventually at some later step in the derivation a property of α is satisfied.

   Using Exceptional Case Marking (ECM) as a test case, let me compare Chomsky's (1994) definition of Greed to the definition of Greediest. I will use the Agr_O theory of clause structure, since that is assumed in Chomsky 1994 and in Chomsky and Lasnik 1993. Consider (5).

(5)
Mary believes John to be in the room.

At some point in the derivation, the structure (6) is formed.

(6)
$[_{T'}$ to be $[_{SC}$ John in the room]]

Given this structure, the next step in the derivation is to raise *John* to the specifier of the infinitival T. The Extended Projection Principle (EPP) holds of the embedded infinitival T, so that if Spec T is not filled overtly the derivation will crash. This movement yields the structure shown in (7).

(7)
$[_{TP}$ John$_i$ $[_{T'}$ to be $[_{SC}$ t$_i$ in the room]]]

On the theory of Case in Chomsky 1993 and Chomsky 1994, where accusative Case is checked by moving a DP into the specifier position of Agr$_O$P at LF, it follows that the DP *John* in (7) has not moved to get its Case checked. In fact, although the EPP is satisfied, there are no morphological properties of *John* (for example, Case or ϕ-features) that are satisfied by the movement of *John* to Spec T, and so Greediest in (4) would be violated. This constitutes the strongest argument against a principle such as Greediest.

Now consider how Chomsky's (1994) Greed would work to explain the movement in (7). Suppose that *John* had not moved, and then the rest of the overt structure were built. This would yield (8).[1]

(8)
$[_{TP}$ Mary T $[_{Agr_OP}$ Agr$_O$ $[_{VP}$ believes $[_{TP}$ to be $[_{SC}$ John in the room]]]]]

The derivation with this structure will crash, since the EPP is not satisfied at Spell-Out for the embedded T. At LF, *John* then raises to Spec Agr$_O$ and has its Case and ϕ-features checked. With movement of the main verb to Agr$_O$ left out, this yields the LF representation (9).

(9)
$[_{TP}$ Mary T $[_{Agr_OP}$ John$_i$ Agr$_O$ $[_{VP}$ believes $[_{TP}$ to be $[_{SC}$ t$_i$ in the room]]]]]

Does this derivation violate the form of Greed given in (3)? It is not obvious that it does or that it does not. In one sense, the features of *John* have been satisfied after movement at LF. In another sense, they have not, since this movement was not part of a convergent derivation (since the EPP has not be satisfied). However, as Chomsky (1993, 1994) makes clear, Last Resort does not select among convergent derivations. Therefore, even if the derivation leading to (9) crashes, this fact by itself should not force overt movement of *John* to the embedded Spec T.

One possibility is that the movement of *John* to Spec Agr$_O$ illustrated in (9) violates the Minimal Link Condition (having skipped the infinitival T, whose specifier would be an A-position), and that a chain violating such a condition is not a legitimate LF object. Under these assumptions, overt movement of *John* into Spec TP would be forced, since otherwise the chain (John, t) would not be a legitimate LF object. This explanation relies crucially on assuming that *John* may not move through the embedded Spec T at LF (since otherwise movement of *John* would not violate the MLC). However, whether or not these assumptions are correct, it is still unclear whether Chomsky's (1994) definition of Greed (see (3) above) is violated, since even though (John, t) would not be a legitimate LF object in (9) (having violated MLC) it is still true that *John* would have its Case and ϕ-features checked.

I will not pursue this issue further. It seems to me that the proposals in Chomsky 1994 and in Chomsky and Lasnik 1993 are interesting, but that there is an easier way to view the issue (as I will show in the next section).

As I pointed out in chapter 1, another criticism (perhaps the most important) of the definition of Greed in Chomsky 1994 is that it is global in a way that can be discerned apart from any particular derivations. Consider moving α at a particular step in the derivation. This is permitted only if not moving α would result in a derivation where the properties of α would not be satisfied (this is the meaning of "otherwise"). But this means that we must look at the derivation where α is not moved, and see what the outcome of that derivation is. Whether the properties of α are satisfied is a global decision.

The definition of Last Resort presented in the next section yields an account of ECM and successive cyclic movement that avoids the problems and questions raised above in regard to Chomsky's (1994) analysis.

5.2   Asymmetric Checking Relations

Consider again the movement of *John* into the Spec of TP in (7). The intuition that I would like to capture is that it is some property of the infinitival *to* that motivates this movement, even if no feature of *John* is checked.

In Collins 1995 I proposed a condition called Greedier. The basic intuition of this condition is that movement of α to the checking domain of a head H need not result in the checking of a feature of α. In this book I have chosen to call this condition Last Resort, since that name is just as accurate as Greedier and more in line with what is becoming standard usage (Lasnik 1995).[2]

The Greedier condition in Collins 1995 is basically equivalent to the definition of Last Resort I gave in chapter 2 and in (1) above, repeated here as (10).

(10)
Move raises α to the checking domain of a head H with a feature F only if the feature F of H enters into a checking relation with a feature F of α.

This definition relies on the notion of checking relation (cf. (2)):

(11)

F1 and F2 enter a checking relation iff F2 is in the checking domain of F1 and F1 is deleted. (F2 may also be deleted.)

Now consider how this definition of Last Resort can be used to explain movement of *John* to the specifier of the infinitival T in (7). First, we have to know what feature of *to* in (7) is being satisfied. In Collins 1995 I assume infinitival *to* to have a null Case feature that must be checked overtly and state that this null Case comes in two varieties: one that checks PRO and one Case that licenses the trace of A-movement (in ECM and raising). These can be represented by T_{PRO} and T_{null}. This assumption basically accepts the postulation of null Case in Chomsky and Lasnik 1993. In addition, we need the following assumption:

(12)

Only a DP with an undeleted Case feature can enter into a checking relation with the null Case of T_{null}.

Under this assumption, the movement in (7) is easy to account for. Consider the definition of Last Resort in (10) applied to movement of *John* in (7). *John* has an accusative Case feature, and *to* has an undeleted null Case feature. As a result of movement of *John* to Spec T, the null Case feature of *to* enters into a checking relation with the accusative Case feature of *John*. In this checking relation, the null Case feature of T is deleted, but not the accusative Case feature of *John*. In other words, what is forcing the movement of *John* is the null Case feature of *to*, not any other feature further up in the tree.

This analysis assumes that the checking relation between *John* and *to* is asymmetrical. In other words: as a result of the establishment of this checking relation, the null Case feature of *to* is deleted but the accusative Case feature of *John* is not.

Watanabe's (1995b) theory of Case checking adds plausibility to the analysis of *to* as assigning two kinds of null Case. On Watanabe's theory, the only thing that differentiates T_{null} and T_{PRO} is the presence of a complementizer.

Note that Greed is not a good name for the condition in (10), since it is not the deletion of a feature of *John* that drives movement. It is for this reason that I use the term Last Resort (for essentially the same reason as Lasnik (1995)).

5.2.1 Interpretable and Uninterpretable Features

Chomsky's (1995, chapter 4) analysis of Last Resort is similar in spirit to the one presented above, in that both rely on the concept of asymmetric feature checking. Chomsky's analysis is arguably superior in several ways. First, Chomsky's treatment (p. 267) eliminates the use of null Case to account for ECM and raising. Second, Chomsky puts the theory of asymmetric feature

checking on a firm foundation by distinguishing interpretable from uninterpretable features and by showing how asymmetric feature checking may be used
in the analysis of constructions in which multiple feature checking occurs (e.g.,
multiple-subject constructions).

I will briefly review Chomsky's analysis here. Except for some minor revisions,
I will basically conclude by accepting Chomsky's arguments. In addition, I will
show how the analysis can be used to explain certain cases of improper movement.

Chomsky (1995: 267) claims that what drives the movement of *John* in (7)
is the EPP feature of the embedded T. This feature is checked against the D
feature of *John*. In Collins 1995 I postulated two types of null Case (T_{PRO} and
T_{null}) and relied on the assumption that checking of null Case could be asymmetric to allow ECM and successive cyclic movement to satisfy Last Resort.
However, given the analysis of locative and quotative inversion (chapter 2), we
know that the EPP feature of T and the Case-assigning feature of T are independent. Therefore, it is preferable not multiply the types of null Case that exist.
Rather, given that T has a strong EPP feature, we can say that in ECM and raising, it is that EPP feature that is being checked in the embedded clause. Therefore,
the force needed to drive raising and ECM can be unified with the independently
needed force needed to drive locative and quotative inversion.

Furthermore, Chomsky formulates asymmetric feature checking in the context of the distinction between interpretable and uninterpretable features. He also
shows how this distinction plays a crucial role in accounting for successive cyclic
movement.[3]

In Chomsky's system, the features that enter into interpretation at LF are interpretable, while the other features are uninterpretable and must be eliminated
for convergence. Consider (13).

(13)
We build airplanes.

According to Chomsky (1995: 278), the operations that interpret this sentence
will have to know that "build" is a verb and "airplanes" is a N. They will also
have to know the φ-features of the N (in order to know how many airplanes there
are).[4] Because there will be no way to interpret the Case feature of the noun
and the agreement feature of "build,"[5] they must be deleted before LF.

Given this characterization of interpretable features, Chomsky categorizes as
interpretable the categorial features (+/–V, +/–N, D, T, etc.), the φ-features of
N (person, number, gender), and the [+*wh*] feature of a *wh*-phrase. He charac-
terizes as uninterpretable the Case features of N, the agreement and Case features of V and T, any strong features, and any other features not listed under
the set of interpretable features.

Working from these assumptions, Chomsky (1995: 280) proposes the following condition:

(14)
A checked feature is deleted when possible.

I interpret this to mean that, if a feature F1 is in the checking domain of F2 (and F1 = F2), then both F1 and F2 delete, if that is possible. Chomsky interprets "possible" in the following way: deletion is possible up to recoverability. This has the consequence that interpretable features (needed in interpretation) are not deletable. On the other hand, uninterpretable features are always "deleted when checked," except if otherwise specified.

According to Chomsky, a deleted feature is not visible to LF, and an erased feature is not accessible to any operation. The distinction between erasure and deletion depends in part on the analysis of multiple-feature-checking structures (such as multiple subjects and serial verb constructions). Since these issues are of no concern in this book, I will simply collapse these two notions here, so that a deleted feature is neither visible at LF nor accessible to any operations.

In this book, I will basically adopt Chomsky's conclusions about the strong EPP feature of T driving movement and the distinction between interpretable and uninterpretable features. However, I do not adopt all of Chomsky's assumptions. In particular, Chomsky assumes that Last Resort and the Minimal Link Condition are incorporated into the definition of Move, and calls this operation Attract (Chomsky 1995: 296, 297). For reasons discussed in chapter 2, I do not take such a position. I will continue under the assumption that Move is simply a Copy and Merge operation and that Last Resort and Minimality are independent economy conditions.

In light of all these assumptions, let us return to how Chomsky's (1995: 345) system (minus the postulation of Attract) can handle ECM. Consider again the following sentence and the relevant level of representation:

(15)
Mary believes John to be in the room.

(16)
$[_{T'}$ to be $[_{SC}$ John in the room$]]$

Why is *John* permitted to raise to the embedded Spec T position? *John* has a D feature, which can enter into a checking relation with the EPP feature of the infinitival T. Because of this, movement of *John* to Spec T satisfies Last Resort. The strong EPP feature of T is deleted. The D feature of *John* may not delete, because it is interpretable, and deleting it would violate recoverability of deletion.

The analysis of successive cyclic A-movement has the same general explanation, according to Chomsky (1995: 283). Consider (17).

(17)
John seems to be in the room.

This sentence involves movement of *John* to the embedded Spec T position, illustrated in (18).

(18)
[$_{TP}$ John$_i$ [$_{T'}$ to be [$_{SC}$ t$_i$ in the room]]]

As in the case of ECM, this movement satisfies Last Resort, since the D feature of *John* enters into a checking relation with the EPP feature of the infinitival T. The strong EPP feature of T is deleted. The D feature of *John* is not deleted, because of recoverability. After this step, the matrix verb and the matrix T are merged into the structure, and *John* is raised to the specifier of the matrix T.

(19)
[$_{TP}$ John$_i$ [$_{T'}$ T [$_{VP}$ seems [$_{TP}$ t$_i$ [$_{T'}$ to be [$_{SC}$t$_i$ in the room]]]]]]

The movement of *John* to the matrix Spec T position satisfies Last Resort because the D feature of *John* enters into a checking relation with the strong EPP feature of the matrix T.

   Chomsky's system has the ability to account for the generalization (Collins 1993: 170) that, while the ϕ-features of a DP may enter into several agreement relations, the Case features of a DP may never enter into several checking relations.

   The following example illustrates this for the Case features of DP: Suppose that the Case features of a DP may enter into multiple checking relations. Now consider (20), where the agreement relations are put aside for simplicity.

(20)
*John$_i$ seems that t$_i$ was singing yesterday.
"It seems that John was singing yesterday."

If the Case feature *John* could enter into two checking relations, then *John* could enter into a checking relation with the Case feature of the embedded T, and subsequently enter into a checking relation with the Case feature of the matrix T. Since the sentence is unacceptable, this is not the case.

   Given that the Case feature of a DP may not enter into several checking relations, the crucial fact is that even if movement of *John* to the matrix Spec T position would satisfy Last Resort (because of the D feature of *John* enters into a checking relation with the EPP feature), the Case feature of the matrix T would remain undeleted.

On the other hand, many languages illustrate the phenomenon of agreement in successive cyclic A-movement. For example, as Carstens (1994), Kinyalolo (1991), and Demuth and Gruber (1994) point out, the Bantu languages allow a single DP to agree with several auxiliaries. This is illustrated in (21) with data from Sesotho (from Demuth and Gruber 1994: 23).[6]

(21)
a. Ke-n-e   n-ka-be   ke-ø-reka
   1sg-cop-pst   1sg-pot-cop   1sg-cont-buy
   "I would have been (now) buying."
b. Ke-n-e   ke-tla-be   ke-ø-reka
   1sg-cop-pst   1sg-irr-cop   1sg-cont-buy
   "I would have been (now) buying (when . . .)."

In each of these examples, there is a main verb and two auxiliaries. Each of the auxiliaries is inflected for agreement with the subject. Demuth and Gruber (1994: 23) argue that each auxiliary (and the VP head by the main verb) is dominated by a TP and an Agr_SP, as in (22),[7] where only the highest T is finite, and has a nominative Case-assigning feature. (Assume furthermore that V raises and adjoins to T, and that T raises and adjoins to Agr_S.)

(22)

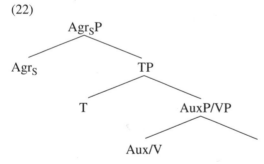

Demuth and Gruber further assume that the multiple-subject agreement in (21) is the result of successive cyclic movement through each Spec Agr_S. In order to reconcile such successive cyclic movement with Greed, they say in their note 20: "We are in accord here with the minimalist conception of Chomsky (1993) that an element can move only to fulfill requirements contingent on its own properties, i.e., operations demonstrate 'Greed'. We might name the quality described here, whereby the operation is driven into a relevant position 'seen' imperfectly at a distance as 'Myopia'. That is, Spec Agr_S are in principle Case, or argument positions, so that A-movement is driven into such positions, even though, when in that position, Case assignment or checking is not attained."

My Last Resort is very similar to Demuth and Gruber's (1994) Myopia. In fact, my formulation of Last Resort was inspired by their condition. They differ only in details and in the intuitions behind them. For me it is necessary that, if a DP moves to the checking domain of H, then a feature of DP and a feature of H must enter into some checking relation, and that the feature of H must delete. For them it is necessary only that the position moved to be a "potential" Case-checking position. This technical difference corresponds to a difference in intuition. In my account, an operation satisfies Last Resort only if some "work" is done (feature deletion). In their account, an operation satisfies Myopia only if some "work" could potentially be done.

Consider how the examples in (21) are accounted for in the theory under consideration. Following Demuth and Gruber (1994), I will give them (leaving out object agreement) the structure shown in (23).

(23)
$[Agr_1 \ T_1 \ Aux_1 \ [Agr_2 \ T_2 \ Aux_2 \ [Agr_3 \ T_3 \ [_{VP} \ DP \ V']]]]$

I assume that the subject DP has both Case and ϕ-features to be checked. When the subject moves into Spec Agr_3P its ϕ-features will enter into a checking relation with the ϕ-features of Agr3. Since the ϕ-features of the DP are interpretable, they do not delete. The ϕ-features of Agr_3 are not interpretable, and therefore they delete. The Case feature of subject DP has not been deleted, since T_3 does not have a Case-assigning feature (by assumption). It is not clear whether the embedded T heads have a strong EPP feature, so that can be left out of consideration here.

Since the subject still has undeleted Case features, it must move. The Agr_2-T_2 complex has uninterpretable ϕ-features to delete, so the next movement of the subject is to Spec Agr_2.[8] The movement of the subject DP to Spec Agr_2 satisfies Last Resort, since the ϕ-features of the subject DP can enter into a checking relation with the ϕ-features of Agr_2. It is important to note that even though the ϕ-features of the DP have entered into a checking relation in Spec Agr_3, movement to the intermediate specifier of Agr_2 is still permitted.[9] Lastly, the subject moves to Spec Agr_1, where its Case and ϕ-features enter into checking relations with the Case and ϕ-features of Agr_1-T_1.

5.3   A′-Movement

Consider the example of long-distance A′-movement shown in (24).

(24)
$[_{CP} \ Who_i \ [_{C'} \ did \ John \ say \ [_{CP} \ t_i \ [_{C'} \ that \ Mary \ liked \ t]]]]$

Assume that movement to the matrix Spec CP is driven by a strong Q feature of the matrix C. Also assume, following Chomsky (1995), that a weak Q feature is interpretable, that a strong Q feature is uninterpretable, and that the [+wh] feature of a wh-phrase is interpretable. In this case, what drives the movement of the wh-phrase into the embedded Spec CP? The movement of *who* to the intermediate Spec CP is not obviously driven by any morphological feature of *who* entering a checking relation.

There is a fact concerning successive cyclic A'-movement that I have ignored up to this point. The fact is that in many languages there are morphological reflexes of successive cyclic A'-movement. In these languages—Irish, Ewe (Collins 1993), Hausa, French—movement through an intermediate Spec causes a morphological change in the intermediate C. This is illustrated below with an example from Irish (McCloskey 1979: 17; see also Chung and McCloskey 1987), where the complementizers are set in boldface to facilitate parsing:

(25)

Deir siad **goN** síleann an t-athair **goN** bpósfaidh Síle é
say they that thinks the father that will marry Sheila him
"They say that the father thinks that Sheila will marry him."

(26)

an fear **aL** deir siad **aL** síleann an t-athair **aL** bpósfaidh Síle
the man that say they that thinks the father that will marry Sheila
"the man that they say the father thinks Sheila will marry."

In Irish the affirmative non-negative non-past complementizer is *goN* (where N stands for nasalization and L stands for lenition). I will assume that *aL* is the complementizer that is used when Spec CP has been filled (this is an idealization of the facts, but it suffices for present purposes). I will assume that there is a strong [+wh] feature on each C that enters into a checking relation with the [+wh] feature of the wh-phrase as it moves through each Spec CP position. This [+wh] feature of C may be distinguished from the Q feature of the matrix C (which acts something like a scope marker), which also must enter into a checking relation with a wh-phrase. The [+wh] feature on C is uninterpretable, since (unlike Q) it does not enter into interpretation.

Given the existence of the [+wh] feature, consider again how the structure in (24) can be derived:

(27)

i. movement to intermediate Spec CP: the strong [+wh] feature of C enters into a checking relation with the wh-phrase.

ii. movement to matrix Spec CP: the strong Q feature of matrix C (along with the strong [+wh] feature) enters into a checking relation with the wh-phrase.

Since a checking relation is established after movement of the *wh*-phrase to the embedded Spec CP, it follows that Last Resort is satisfied in successive cyclic movement.

Many questions remain. For example, we must evidently assume that generating a C with a strong [+*wh*] feature is optional to account for embedded clauses of declarative sentences (where no A′-movement has occurred). In other words, the complementizer in (28) may not have a strong [+*wh*] feature, since otherwise the derivation would crash.

(28)
I said that John left.

A related question is whether successive cyclic movement is obligatory. For example, we assumed that movement through the intermediate Spec CP was necessary in the derivation in (24), and we saw how such movement satisfies Last Resort. Indeed, in Irish movement through all the embedded Spec C positions seems necessary to account for the data (J. McCloskey, personal communication). There are, however, languages which suggest that movement through all the intermediate Spec CP positions is not required.

This can be illustrated by means of some examples from Ewe.[10] First, consider the paradigm (29), which shows that the form of the nominative pronoun depends on whether or not Spec C is filled.

(29)
é/*wò   ƒo   Kɔsi
3sg   hit   Kosi
"He hit Kosi."

(30)
Kofi   gblɔ   be   é/*wò   ƒo   Kɔsi
Kofi   said   P   3sg   hit   Kosi
"Kofi said that he hit Kosi."

(31)
Kofi   biɛ   be   lamata   *é/wò   ƒo   Kɔsi
Kofi   asked   P   why   3sg   hit   Kosi
"Kofi asked why he hit Kosi."

Example (29) indicates that *é* occurs in matrix indicative clauses and *wò* does not. Example (30) indicates that the third singular subject of an embedded clause can only be *é*; it cannot be *wò*. Example (31) indicates that if there has been movement into Spec CP in the embedded clause, then *wò* is obligatory. This is analyzed in Collins 1993 as follows: If Spec of CP is occupied (as in (31), but not

(29) or (30)), a special form of nominative Case is assigned to the subject of the associated TP. It is this special form of nominative Case that accounts for the appearance of *wò* in (29). The details of this process are not relevant to our present concerns.

Interestingly, if there is A′-movement out of an embedded clause, the pronoun *wò* is not obligatory in the embedded clause, as (32) and (33) show.[11]

(32)

Kɔsi	ɛ	me	gblɔ	be	é/wò	fo
Kosi	foc	I	said	C	he	hit

"Kosi, I said that he hit."

(33)

me	e	gblɔ	be	é/wò	fo
who	you	say	C	3sg	hit

"Who did you say that he hit?"

It would be nice to obtain data involving further embedded clauses. Unfortunately, extraction out of more than one embedded clause is generally somewhat degraded (whether *wò* is selected or not), so we will have to assume that (32) and (33) are representative. With successive cyclic movement, the structure of the embedded Spec C in these clauses would be as shown in (34).

(34)

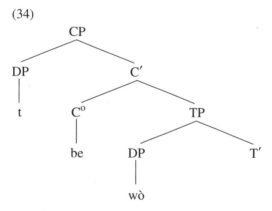

Under the assumption of successive cyclic movement, it is hard to see why selection of *wò* should be optional in (32) and (33) but obligatory in (31). One possibility is that successive cyclic movement is not obligatory in Ewe. Under this analysis, the Ewe facts could be accounted for as follows. For movement out of an embedded clause, if the embedded C has a strong [+wh] feature, then movement through the embedded Spec C is obligatory (and satisfies Last Resort), and the pronoun *wò* is selected. If the embedded C has no [+wh] feature, then the *wh*-phrase may not move to the embedded Spec CP position (such movement would violate Last Resort). Therefore, *wò* is not selected.[12]

This account leaves unexplained the difference between Irish (successive cyclic movement obligatory) and Ewe (successive cyclic movement optional).[13] It strikes me that a comprehensive survey of languages showing such reflexes of successive cyclicity would have to be conducted before such an account could be attempted.

One consequence of my formulation of Last Resort is that intermediate adjunction will never be possible, since intermediate adjunction involves no feature-checking relation. Consider the derivation yielding an intermediate adjunction structure, as in (35).

(35)
$[_{CP}$ who$_i$ $[_{C'}$ $[_{VP}$ t$_i$ $[_{VP}$ t$_i]]]]$

Suppose that in this case there has been adjunction to the category VP, yielding the complex category [VP, VP]. If we assume that V has no feature that can enter into a feature-checking relation with *who* in the VP-adjoined position, then this adjunction will not be allowed.[14] In fact, it is highly unlikely that any intermediate adjunction results in the establishment of a feature-checking relation. This gives rise to the following speculation (see Collins 1994d):

(36)
There is no intermediate adjunction.

5.4 Form Chain

It is clear that, on the above account of successive cyclic movement, the operation of Form Chain may be dispensed with. Chomsky (1993: 15) proposed the operation of Form Chain to account for a dilemma posed by the theory of economy: the dilemma between the principle that the shortest movement operation is always chosen and the notion that the derivation with the fewest operations blocks other derivations. In this light, consider the representations in (37), which are from Chomsky 1993: 15.

(37)
a. $[_{TP1}$ e seems $[_{TP2}$ e to be likely $[_{TP3}$ John to win]]]
b. $[_{TP1}$ John seems $[_{TP2}$ t$'$ to likely $[_{TP3}$ t to win]]]

Movement of *John* directly to the matrix Spec TP position would involve the fewest steps (one movement). Successive cyclic movement, illustrated in (37b), would involve more but smaller steps. In order to resolve the conflict between

Shortest Move and Fewest Steps, Chomsky proposed a Form Chain operation that applies to the structure in (37a), and produces the structure in (37b). Therefore, there is simply one operation of Form Chain in (37b), and the links of the resulting chain are minimal.

Under local economy, there is no notion of economy that chooses the derivation with the fewest steps. Therefore, whether (37b) involves one instance of Form Chain or two is irrelevant. What is important is that all operations satisfy Last Resort. Suppose that there is no operation Form Chain. In that case, movement of *John* to Spec T_2 satisfies Last Resort, since the EPP feature of the embedded T_2 enters into a checking relation with the D feature of *John*. Similarly, movement of *John* to Spec T_1 satisfies Last Resort, since the EPP feature of T_1 enters into a checking relation with the D feature of *John*.

Given the definition of Last Resort in (1), it seems that the minimal hypothesis is that there is no need for a notion of Form Chain. Therefore, we can abandon it.

Even though there is no operation of Form Chain, it is still necessary to have some notion of chain. The simple reason is that chains are needed for interpretation at LF. A chain may act as an argument, such that the θ-role of a verb is assigned to a chain. Therefore, even though I do not have an operation of Form Chain, let me maintain (modifying Chomsky and Lasnik 1993) that there is a way to link chains.[15]

(38)   *Chain-Formation Principle 1*
Let C_1 and C_2 be two member chains of the following forms (assuming the copy theory of movement), where $a_2 = b_1$: $C_1 = (a_1, a_2)$ and $C_2 = (b_1, b_2)$. Suppose that a_1 (the head of C_1) has a feature F that enters into a checking relation. Then, if b_1 has the same feature F that enters into a checking relation, the chains C_1 and C_2 may be linked to form C3 $= (a_1, a_2, b_2)$.

This definition ensures that a linked chain is not formed from links that have completely different characteristics. In other words, if both C_1 and C_2 are formed by the need for the D feature of a DP to enter a checking relation, then C_1 and C_2 may be linked. The resulting chains will be used in the interpretational component.

There may remain other reasons to adopt a notion of Form Chain. For example, it is argued in Collins 1994a and in Takahashi 1994 that the ban on chain interleaving provides evidence for an operation of Form Chain. However, Müller (1994) argues that chain interleaving does in fact exist, which suggests that there is no operation of Form Chain. In this book I will not assume that there is an operation Form Chain. However, there are remnants of this operation in the guise of chain-formation principles. The first of these remnants was Chain-Formation Principle 1, given above.

5.4.1 Partial *Wh*-Movement in English

Although I assume that there is no operation of Form Chain, there is still some reason to retain the concept *chain* discussed above. In addition, I will show in this section (and in section 5.5, and in chapter 6) that there are other principles that refer to the notion of *incomplete chain*.

Given that an embedded C may have a strong [+*wh*] feature, we must ask why (39) is not acceptable in English.

(39)
*Who thinks what John saw?
"Who thinks that John saw what?"

In this sentence, the embedded C has, by hypothesis, a strong [+*wh*] feature. Therefore, movement of *what* to the embedded Spec C satisfies Last Resort. This sentence cannot be ruled out as violating the selectional requirements of *thinks*. At LF, the *wh*-phrase *what* will not be interpreted as being in the Spec CP of an embedded question (as indicated by the gloss).

Epstein (1992: 249) proposes an economy account that would rule out (39). The ultimate derivation of this sentence will involve two operations: one to move *what* to the embedded Spec CP at S-Structure and one to move *what* to the matrix Spec CP at LF. According to Epstein, there is a shorter derivation involving a one-step movement of *what* from the object position of *saw* to the matrix Spec CP at LF (assuming no subjacency at LF). This shorter derivation blocks the longer two-step derivation by economy.

Clearly this reasoning is not allowed in our system, since it involves a global economy calculation. A derivation with one step wins over a derivation with two steps.

I will propose a local condition that has the same effect as Epstein's analysis. First, assume that interpreting *wh-in-situ* involves no LF movement. Consider (40).

(40)
who likes what

I am suggesting that in order to interpret this it is not necessary to move *what* to a specifier of the matrix C. (See Reinhart 1995 for much discussion of this point.) It is immaterial for our purposes how *wh-in-situ* is actually interpreted.

Given this assumption, we can conclude that the *wh*-phrase in (39) does not move to the matrix Spec CP position at LF. Therefore, the chain (what, t) that has been formed in (39) will never be completed by moving *what* to the matrix Spec C. I suggest that this is the problem with (39). Let us formalize this as in (41).[16]

(41)   *Chain-Formation Principle 2*
At LF, no incomplete chains are allowed.

This definition rests on the notion of incomplete chain, given in (42).[17]

(42)
Let Ch be a (nontrivial) chain of the form $(\alpha, \ldots, t)$, where α has a $[+wh]$
feature that has entered into a checking relation with a $[+wh]$ feature but has
not entered into a checking relation with Q. Then Ch is an incomplete chain.

In effect this definition says that, although the movement to form a intermediate link in a chain may be driven to check the $[+wh]$ feature of C, the real reason for movement is to check the Q feature of a C.[18]

How does this definition apply to (39)? In this representation, the chain (what,
t) is incomplete, since *what* has entered into a checking relation with a $[+wh]$ C
but has not yet entered into a checking relation with Q. In addition, *what* will
never enter into a checking relation with Q, since I have postulated that there is
no LF *wh*-movement. Therefore, partial *wh*-movement gives rise to an incomplete chain at LF.[19]

Is Chain-Formation Principle 2 local? Since it is verified at one particular
stage (LF), it is local. One potential problem with (41) is that in order to evaluate whether a chain is incomplete we must look at the checking relations that the
links in the chain have established. For example, we must verify whether a *wh*-
phrase has entered a checking relation with a $[+wh]$ C at LF. Since we have assumed that deleted features are invisible to LF conditions and to internal
operations, this looks problematic. I will leave it for further work on the nature
of feature checking to resolve this.[20]

5.5   Improper Movement

The formulation of Last Resort also rules out most cases of improper movement.
Consider the classical example (43).

(43)
*John$_i$ was expected [$_{CP}$ t$_i$ [$_{C'}$ that it was told t$_i$ that Mary left]]
"It was expected that John was told that Mary left."

The standard account of this sentence is in terms of condition C (May 1979).
The account based on condition C is problematic in that the intermediate trace
left by *John* in Spec CP need not be present at LF (it may simply be deleted).[21]

An alternative analysis of (43) is that it violates Last Resort. Since *John* has
no $[+wh]$ feature, there is no reason for it to move through the embedded Spec

CP position. To put it another way, suppose that the embedded C has a strong [+*wh*] feature. Since *John* is not a *wh*-phrase, movement of *John* to the embedded Spec C would violate Last Resort. Therefore, the lack of improper movement in English constitutes strong support for Last Resort.[22]

Now consider the slightly more complicated example (44).

(44)
*[$_{CP}$ who$_i$ [$_{TP}$ t$_i''$ was expected [$_{CP}$ t$_i'$ [$_{C'}$ that it was told t$_i$ that Mary left]]]]
a. *who* moves to embedded Spec C (from the complement position of *told*)
b. *who* moves from embedded Spec C to matrix Spec T
c. *who* moves from Spec T to the matrix Spec C.

This example differs from (43) only in that the element that undergoes movement is *who* instead of *John*. Step (44a) satisfies Last Resort since *who* has a [+*wh*] feature, and *who* may enter into a checking relation with the [+*wh*] feature of the embedded C. Since the [+*wh*] feature of *who* is interpretable, it is not deleted in the checking relation. Since the [+*wh*] feature of the embedded C is uninterpretable, it is deleted.

The operation in (44b) satisfies Last Resort since *who* has a D feature that may enter into a checking relation with the strong EPP feature of T.

The operation in (44c) satisfies Last Resort since *who* has a [+*wh*] feature, that can enter into a checking relation with the strong Q feature of the matrix C and the strong [+*wh*] feature of the matrix C.

The derivation in (44) must be ruled out, since the sentence is unacceptable. It is easy to verify that each of the movement operations in (44) satisfies Minimality, so that condition is not being violated. One way to rule this out is to appeal to a stipulation that the trace of A′-movement must be Case marked (i.e., "variables must be Case marked"). This stipulation is clearly not permitted in the minimalist framework. Every constituent X must have its uninterpretable features deleted. If they are deleted, the derivation converges.

I suggest that (44) can be ruled out by a chain-formation principle. This principle basically states that there is no chain interleaving (see Collins 1994a for related discussion). In other words, the derivation in (44) is unacceptable, since it involves constructing part of one chain (the A′-chain), switching to the A-chain, then switching back to the A′-chain. Let us call this Chain-Formation Principle 3.

(45)   *Chain-Formation Principle 3*
Let Ch be an incomplete chain (α, . . . , t). The movement of α may only add another link to Ch.

The definition of incomplete chain is given in (42), and the definition of Chain Linking in (38). To see how (45) works, consider the derivation in (44) again. The operation in (44a) satisfies Last Resort. In addition, when *who* is *in situ* it forms a trivial chain. Therefore, the movement in (44a) does not violate Chain-Formation Principle 3.

The operation in (44b) satisfies Last Resort. The *wh*-phrase has a D feature, and this feature enters into a checking relation with the matrix T, which has a strong EPP feature. On the other hand, this movement violates Chain-Formation Principle 3. Before the operation in (44b), the chain (who, t) had been formed by movement of *who* to the embedded Spec C position. This forms an incomplete chain, since the [+*wh*] feature of *who* has not entered into a checking relation with a (strong) Q. Therefore, since the movement in (44b) does not add a link to the chain (who, t), it is ruled out.

Actually, it seems that Chain-Formation Principle 3 can be derived from Chain-Formation Principles 1 and 2. Consider again, the operation in (44b). This operation cannot add a link to (who, t), which was formed in (44a), because of Chain-Formation Principle 1 (see (38)). Similarly, the operation in (44c) cannot add a link to (who, t), because of Chain-Formation Principle 1 (38) again. Therefore, (who, t) is incomplete, which is ruled out by Chain-Formation Principle 2 (see (41)).

There are global alternatives to this treatment.[23] Consider the analysis of Takahashi (1994: 113). Suppose that we have the condition on Form Chain shown in (46).

(46)
An operation of Form Chain must be a collection of instances of the same type (A or A$'$ movement).

Given this condition, consider the derivation in (44). The operation in (44a), forms the chain (who$_i$, t$_i$), where *who* is in the embedded Spec CP. The operation in (44b) forms a different chain (who$_i$, t$_i$), where *who* is in Spec T. The operation in (44c) forms yet a third chain (who$_i$, t$_i$), where *who* is in the matrix Spec CP. Therefore, the derivation in (88) involves three operations of Form Chain. Now consider the derivation shown in (47).

(47)
a. *who* moves from the complement position of *told* to the matrix Spec T.
b. *who* moves from the matrix Spec T, to the matrix Spec CP.

This derivation only takes two operations; therefore, according to the economy condition requiring the fewest steps, it is preferred over the three-chain derivation.

The derivation in (47) involves a violation of Minimality, since the expletive *it* intervenes between the complement position of *told* and the matrix Spec T position. Since the least costly derivation involves a violation of Minimality (or the Shortest Move Condition), the sentence is ruled out.

Takahashi's approach is conceptually very similar to mine involving Chain-Formation Principle 3. The difference is that Takahashi must appeal to global economy. In other words, derivations are compared on the basis of overall cost. In my formulation, each step in the derivation is evaluated for cost, and each step is constrained (locally) by the Chain-Formation Principles.

Many other cases of improper movement are also blocked by Last Resort. For example, intermediate adjunction of a verb to a maximal projection would not be possible, since (as was assumed in (36)) intermediate adjunction to a maximal projection does not result in feature checking.

5.6 Conclusion

This chapter has provided independent justification for the principle of Last Resort that was given in chapter 2. This definition is repeated as (48).

(48)
Move raises α to the checking domain of a head H with a feature F only if the feature F of H enters into a checking relation with a feature F of α.

The main justifications for this particular formulation of Last Resort are the following: First, this definition of Last Resort is local. Whether an operation applying to a set of representations Σ satisfies Last Resort can be decided on the basis of information in Σ. Second, this definition, supplemented with the notion of asymmetric feature checking (Collins 1994d, 1995), allows me to account for ECM and successive cyclic movement. Third, using this definition of Last Resort, I can account for cases of improper movement.

This definition of Last Resort also allows me to eliminate the notion of Form Chain, which was motivated by considerations of global economy . However, this result is less spectacular than it may seem to be, since I found it necessary to introduce Chain-Formation Principles 1–3. One more Chain-Formation Principle will be introduced in chapter 6.

Chapter 6
Procrastinate

Procrastinate is the one global economy condition that has not yet been analyzed in any detail. In this chapter, I will reanalyze some of the data which Procrastinate has been used in explaining.

The results of this chapter will be less ambitious than those of the other chapters, since I cannot show that the effects of Procrastinate reduce to independently motivated conditions (as I did with the strict cycle in chapter 4). However, I will suggest ways in which Procrastinate may be eliminated in favor of more local treatments.

There are basically three areas in which Procrastinate has been used in explaining syntactic phenomena: it has been used to help explain differences between verb movement in French and English, in explaining the unacceptability of certain expletive constructions, and in explaining certain properties of multiple-subject constructions in Icelandic. In particular, Chomsky (1995: 375) assumes that T in Icelandic may be specified as being strong and admitting a single unforced violation of Procrastinate. For reasons of space, I will not deal with this third case in this book. Verb movement in French and English is discussed immediately below, and expletive constructions are discussed in section 6.2.

Chomsky (1993) proposed Procrastinate in order to help explain a paradigm involving verb movement in French and English. The relevant examples (from Pollock 1989) are given in (1) and (2).

(1)
a. *John kisses often Mary.
b. John often kisses Mary.

(2)
a. Jean embrasse souvent Marie.
b. *Jean souvent embrasse Marie.

If it is assumed that the adverb occupies some position (adjoined or specifier) between T and V, this paradigm can be described in the following way: In English, the verb cannot raise to T; in French, the verb must raise to T.

Chomsky (1993: 30) proposes to account for this paradigm in terms of feature strength. In French the V feature of T is strong; in English the V feature of T is weak. Chomsky assumes that strong features are visible at PF and weak features are not. On the other hand, syntactic features are not legitimate PF objects (unlike the feature [labial], or some other phonological feature). Therefore, if the strong V feature of T in French is not checked (or deleted), it will cause the derivation to crash. Therefore, the verb raises in French to ensure convergence.

Since the V feature of T is weak in English, the verb does not have to raise. What forces it to stay *in situ*? Chomsky proposes that an economy principle he calls Procrastinate states that covert operations are less costly than overt operations. Chomsky (1994: 428) also assumes that Procrastinate selects among the set of convergent derivations. In other words, if overt movement is not forced by convergence it is barred.

Procrastinate has a different feel than the other economy conditions. It has never been proposed that either Last Resort or Minimality can be violated when not doing so would result in a nonconvergent derivation. Furthermore, Procrastinate introduces a curious non-uniformity into the derivation. The derivation is characterized as a mapping from the Numeration (or a set of lexical choices) to LF. Spell-Out applies to some intermediate representation and initiates the PF branch. Given this characterization, there is no reason to assume that the operations before Spell-Out should be different from those after Spell-Out. In other words, the derivation mapping N to LF is uniform (see Chomsky 1994: 394). If there is a principle such as Procrastinate, uniformity cannot hold: Procrastinate states that covert operations are less costly than overt operations.

The most important argument against Procrastinate is that it is global. Consider the derivation of the French example in (2). At some point in the derivation, the structure shown in (3) will be formed.

(3)

[$_{TP}$ T ADV [$_{VP}$ V DP]]

At this point in the derivation, a decision must be made as to whether to apply verb movement. Procrastinate says that verb movement is possible only if the derivation would not converge otherwise. In order to determine whether the derivation converges, we must look at the derivation at LF and PF to see if there are unchecked features. If there is an unchecked strong feature at PF, the derivation crashes (see Chomsky 1993).

Therefore, we have three reasons to reject Procrastinate: it is not like the other economy conditions, it introduces a non-uniformity into the derivation, and it is nonlocal. Given these considerations, how can we account for (1) and (2)?

The central fact to be explained is that a weak feature may not be checked overtly. Let us assume that weak features may be checked only by pure features. A pure feature is defined as a feature that is not part of any lexical item, where a lexical item is defined as a set {S, F, P} of semantic, formal, and phonetic features. In other words, checking a weak feature F of a head H requires a very strict locality relation between F and the feature F′ with which F enters into a checking relation. In order for F to be checked, F′ itself must be adjoined to H (not merely a lexical item containing F′).

Chomsky (1995: 263) proposes that there is an asymmetry between overt movement and covert movement in that only covert movement allows a feature to move away from its lexical item. Chomsky (1995: 263) gives several reasons why a feature moving away from its phonological matrix overtly would cause the derivation to crash at PF. For example, he suggests that there is a morphological requirement that the features of a single lexical item be within a single head at PF.

Given Chomsky's proposal and my definition of weak feature as one that can only check a pure feature (one that is not part of a lexical item), it follows directly that weak features will be checked only by covert movement. In summary, we have the definitions in (4).

(4)
a. strong feature: a feature that is visible at PF
b. weak feature: a feature that may be checked only by a pure feature

There is no hint of global economy here, since economy of derivation plays no role in determining where in a derivation a weak feature will be checked.[1]

In (1a), the verb moves to T. Since movement must satisfy Last Resort, the tense feature of V has to enter into a checking relation with T. But the V feature of T is weak, so it cannot enter into a checking relation with any feature of V that is still a part of the V "kisses" (which is a lexical item). In (1b), there is no movement, so the weak feature of T does not enter into a checking relation at PF. At LF, the tense feature of V raises and adjoins to T (as do any other formal features). In (2a), there is overt verb movement. The movement must satisfy Last Resort, so V enters into a checking relation with T. This is acceptable, since the V feature of T is strong. In (2b), there is no verb movement. The V feature of T is strong, and so the derivation crashes. Given this analysis, consider (5).

(5)
John is not a teacher.

In this example the auxiliary verb *is* has moved from the V position to adjoin to T. Given that the V feature of T is weak, one may expect (5) to be unacceptable. How can this be accounted for in my system? Although the verb has adjoined to T in (5), it is not clear that it has entered into a checking relation with T. Usually (as in (1) and (2)), when a verb moves it does so in order to enter a checking relation with some functional head, thereby satisfying Last Resort. On the other hand, if auxiliaries (and perhaps other clitic-like elements) were independently motivated to move, movement of the auxiliary in (5) would not need to establish a checking relation, and Last Resort would not be violated.

I suggest that tensed auxiliaries in English must raise in order to be within a word at Morphology: $[_T \text{ AUX T}]$. That this does not follow from checking theory is evidenced by the fact that tensed main verbs do not behave in the same way. This condition is cross-linguistically variable. It does not apply for auxiliaries in Mainland Scandinavian, where auxiliaries do not raise to T in embedded clauses (Watanabe 1993b: 190). This condition is analogous to the condition that has been postulated to account for overt clitic movement: a clitic must adjoin to a functional head overtly. This fact about clitic pronouns has been noted by many people, most recently Diesing (1994a,b), Cardinaletti and Starke (1994), and Chomsky (1994). The phenomenon is being hotly debated, and the accounts given are not mutually consistent. I will simply assume that whatever will eventually account for the overt movement of clitics and auxiliaries is not related to feature strength.

One interesting implication of my definition of weak features is the following: Recall that a strong feature is one that is visible at PF, whereas a weak feature is one that must be checked by a pure feature (i.e., one that is not contained in a lexical item). The fact that these two definitions are independent allows them to be cross-classified. Therefore, we may expect a feature that is neither strong nor weak. This would be a feature that is not visible at PF and that does not have to be checked by a pure feature. Since no Procrastinate condition is being assumed here, such a feature would have the property that it could be checked by either overt or covert movement. This, in turn, would give rise to the appearance of optional movement. I suggest that this may be what accounts for the optionality of object shift, illustrated by (8) in chapter 2. In other words, in Icelandic and other languages that exhibit optional object shift, the D feature of Tr is neither weak nor strong. I suspect that many cases of optional movement may be analyzed in this light.[2] If these tentative suggestions turn out to be right, they support the claims of chapters 1–3 that optionality is more comprehensible under local economy than under global economy (including both the Shortest Derivation Requirement and Procrastinate).

I am not claiming to have answered all the questions concerning Procrastinate, or other "timing" principles.[3] The above account can be mainly taken to highlight what the real problems with Procrastinate are.

6.1   Pied-Piping

In this section, I will consider an alternative approach to Procrastinate found in Chomsky 1995 (p. 262) and show that it too is global. Chomsky proposes the economy condition shown here as (6).

(6)
F carries along just enough material for convergence.[4]

Under this economy condition, covert movement involves just the movement of formal features. For example, LF object shift of a DP is in reality movement of the formal features of the DP (Case, ϕ-features, and D) to adjoin to some functional head.

Overt movement, on the other hand, must pied-pipe some phonological material to ensure convergence. As was mentioned above, Chomsky (1995: 263) proposes that a feature may not be moved away from its lexical item overtly.

As Chomsky makes very clear, only the convergent derivations are considered in finding the optimal derivation. Raising of features (without pied-piping of a phonological matrix) is more economical, but if such raising does not result it a convergent derivation it does not count as a more optimal derivation.

Chomsky (citing Hisa Kitahara and Howard Lasnik) points out that the proposed condition accounts for Procrastinate, since moving a bare feature (no pied-piping) is the least costly operation according to (6). If moving of a bare feature is possible only for covert movement, then covert movement is less costly than overt movement.

However, the principle in (6), with its reliance on the notion of convergence, is highly global. To see this, suppose that we want to raise DP from Spec VP to Spec T, before Spell-Out. This would satisfy Last Resort, since the EPP feature and the Case feature of T are entering into checking relations. According to the principle in (6) it is preferable to move FF(DP) (i.e., Case, ϕ-features, and D) to adjoin to T if this would not cause the derivation to crash. In other words, in order to decide whether we move DP or FF(DP), we must make reference to what happens at PF and not simply to the information available at the current step in the derivation.

Therefore, according to local economy, (6) must be rejected. However, the theory of LF movement of features may be maintained: Let α be a constituent,

and let FF(α) be its formal features. At any point in the derivation, either α or
FF(α) may undergo movement. If FF(α) undergoes movement before Spell-Out,
the derivation will crash, since a feature may not be separated from its lexical
item before PF (as outlined above). If α undergoes movement at LF in order
for some feature F' of α to enter into a checking relation with a weak feature F,
the derivation will crash, since weak features may be checked only by pure
features. There is no principle that states that pied-piping is not preferred. This
is a welcome result, since sentences such as those in (7) show that pied-piping
is optional (which is surprising, on Chomsky's theory).[5]

(7)
a. Which piece of paper did Betty draw on?
b. ?On which piece of paper did Betty draw?

6.2   Expletive Constructions

The other major application of Procrastinate is to expletive constructions
(Chomsky 1994: 428; Chomsky 1995: 346).[6] Chomsky considers the paradigm shown here as (8) and (9).

(8)
a. There seems to be a man in the room.
b. *There seems a man to be in the room.

(9)
a. *Mary believes to be a man in the room.
b. Mary believes a man to be in the room.

At one point in the derivation, the two sentences in (8) share the structure shown
in (10), where SC indicates a small clause.

(10)
[$_{T'}$ to be [$_{SC}$ a man in the room]]

Both sentences in (8) involve the expletive *there*, so we assume that the element *there* is in the Numeration. Given this assumption, there are two possible
operations on the structure in (8): either *a man* may be moved to Spec T, or *there*
may be selected from the Numeration and merged into Spec T. Raising violates Procrastinate, since it is not needed for convergence. Therefore, the expletive *there* is inserted, as shown in (11).

(11)
[$_{TP}$ there [$_{T'}$ to be [$_{SC}$ a man in the room]]]

After merging this structure with the matrix verb and T, we obtain (12).

(12)
[$_{T'}$ T [$_{VP}$ seems [$_{TP}$ there [$_{T'}$ to be [$_{SC}$ a man in the room]]]]]

At this point the only legitimate operation is raising *there* to occupy Spec T (fulfilling the EPP property of T). Raising of *a man* to Spec T would violate the Minimal Link Condition, and so Attract/Move would be undefined.

This explanation involves many assumptions that my theory will not support. For example, it crucially involves the Numeration, to make sure the two derivations are comparable. It also involves Procrastinate, in a very global way. To see this, consider again the options available at the step illustrated in (10). We can raise *a man* only if later in the derivation (at PF) we ascertain that the derivation is nonconvergent. Since this information is not available in (10), the decision is global.

The sentences in (9) are structurally similar to those in (8), so it is surprising that the judgments are just the opposite. Raising of *a man* in the embedded clause is obligatory. Consider Chomsky's (1995: 347) explanation. At some point in the derivation forming the sentences in (9) we have the structure (13).

(13)
[$_{T'}$ to be [$_{SC}$ a man in the room]]

Since both sentences in (9) include the word *Mary*, it is in the Numeration shared by the derivations for these sentences. Given this Numeration, there are (at least) two ways to fill the Spec T position: either *a man* may be moved to Spec T, or *Mary* may be selected from the Numeration and merged into Spec T. By Procrastinate, inserting *Mary* is preferred if it leads to a convergent derivation. The only way that this can be decided is to insert *Mary* and see if the derivation converges. This yields (14).

(14)
[$_{TP}$ Mary [$_{T'}$ to be [$_{SC}$ a man in the room]]]

Next, the matrix verb and T are merged in. Then *Mary* is raised (just was the expletive was raised in (12)) to yield (15).

(15)
[$_{TP}$ Mary$_i$ [$_{T'}$ T [$_{VP}$ believes [$_{TP}$ t$_i$ [$_{T'}$ to be [$_{SC}$ a man in the room]]]]]]

In this structure, the chain (Mary, t) is formed when *Mary* raises from the embedded subject position to the matrix subject position. This chain lacks a θ-role, and Chomsky proposes that this lack of a θ-role causes the derivation to crash. This accounts for the unacceptability of (9a).

Since inserting *Mary* in the structure in (13) eventually causes the derivation to crash, and since Procrastinate selects among convergent derivations, raising of *a man* in structure (13) does not violate Procrastinate, and we derive (16).

(16)
[$_{TP}$ a man$_i$ [$_{T'}$ to be [$_{SC}$ t$_i$ in the room]]]

After this point, the rest of the operations needed to derive (9b) apply.

Note again that this analysis rests on assumptions that I have rejected. For example, it rests squarely on global economy and on the notion that a violation of the θ-Criterion leads to nonconvergence. These sentences constitute the only other strong support (other than (1) and (2)) for Procrastinate that I am aware of.

Consider how the paradigm in (8) and (9) may be analyzed with local economy. Recall that there is no Procrastinate, global economy or Numeration. In addition, Merge is motivated by Integration. If merging a constituent and moving a constituent both satisfy Last Resort and Minimality, they are equally costly. With these assumptions in mind, consider the sentences repeated here as (17).

(17)
a. There seems to be a man in the room.
b. *There seems a man to be in the room.

At one point in the derivation of these sentences, we will have the structure shown in (18).

(18)
[$_{T'}$ to be [$_{SC}$ a man in the room]]

At this point, there are two possible operations. First, *a man* may be copied and merged into Spec T. This operation satisfies Last Resort, since *a man* checks the EPP feature of the infinitival T. Second, *there* may be inserted in Spec TP. This satisfies Last Resort, since the Integration property of *there* is satisfied. Therefore, we have two possible continuations of (18), shown in (19).

(19)
a. [$_{TP}$ there [$_{T'}$ to be [$_{SC}$ a man in the room]]]
b. [$_{TP}$ a man$_i$ [$_{T'}$ to be [$_{SC}$ t$_i$ in the room]]]

This is entirely analogous to the paradigm shown here as (20), which was analyzed in chapter 3.

(20)
a. A man is in the room.
b. There is a man in the room.

As was pointed out in chapter 3, from a global perspective the derivations of the two sentences in (20) do not compete, since they do not have the same Numeration. From the standpoint of local economy, these sentences present no problem. After the matrix T′ has been formed, either inserting *there* or raising *a man* is possible, since both satisfy Last Resort (and Minimality, trivially).

Now consider the continuations of the two structures in (19). After merging the matrix verb and T, we have the structures shown in (21).

(21)
a. [$_{T'}$ T [$_{VP}$ seems [$_{TP}$ there [$_{T'}$ to be [$_{SC}$ a man in the room]]]]]]
b. [$_{T'}$ T [$_{VP}$ seems [$_{TP}$ a man$_i$ [$_{T'}$ to be [$_{SC}$ t$_i$ in the room]]]]]]

One possible step, continuing these derivations, is to raise *there* in (21a) and to raise *a man* in (21b). Both of these operations satisfy Last Resort. Raising *there* checks the EPP feature of the matrix T; raising *a man* checks the EPP feature and Case feature of the matrix T. This leads to the structures (22a) and (22b), which yield, respectively, (23a) and (23b).

(22)
a. [$_{TP}$ there$_k$ [$_{T'}$ T [$_{VP}$ seems [$_{TP}$ t$_k$ [$_{T'}$ to be [$_{SC}$ a man in the room]]]]]]]
b. [$_{TP}$ a man [$_{T'}$ T [$_{VP}$ seems [$_{TP}$ t$_i$ [$_{T'}$ to be [$_{SC}$ t$_i$ in the room]]]]]]]

(23)
a. There seems to be a man in the room.
b. A man seems to be in the room.

A different continuation of the structure in (21b) would have been to insert *there* in the matrix Spec T. This satisfies Last Resort, since the Integration property of *there* is satisfied. This would yield the structure (24).

(24)
[$_{TP}$ there [$_{T'}$ T [$_{VP}$ seems [$_{TP}$ a man$_i$ [$_{T'}$ to be [$_{SC}$ t$_i$ in the room]]]]]]]

This structure is allowed by local economy, so in this case local economy overgenerates. Given that the minimal theory of economy that I have developed so far cannot succeed, I suggest that there is an additional principle of economy that in part captures the intuition that movement is done in order to form chains (not just to satisfy Last Resort). This condition bears a family resemblance to Chain-Formation Principles 1–3 of chapter 5, so I will call it Chain-Formation Principle 4.

(25) *Chain-Formation Principle 4*
If there are two operations OP$_1$ and OP$_2$ applicable to a set of representations Σ (both satisfying Last Resort and Minimality), then choose the operation that extends an incomplete chain.

In order to complete this definition, we must define *complete* and *incomplete chain* for movement that is driven by Case checking and D checking (A-movement). This is completely analogous to the definition of incomplete chain from chapter 5, given here as (26a).

(26)
a. Let Ch be a (nontrivial) chain of the form $(\alpha, \ldots, t)$, where α has a $[+wh]$ feature that has entered into a checking relation with a $[+wh]$ feature but has not entered into a checking relation with Q. Then Ch is an incomplete chain.
b. Let Ch be a (nontrivial) chain of the form $(\alpha, \ldots, t)$, where α has D feature that has entered into a checking relation with a EPP feature and has an unchecked Case feature. Then Ch is an incomplete chain.[7]

This definition says that, although the movement to form a intermediate link may involve the $[+wh]$ feature of C or the EPP feature of T, the primary motivation for forming a chain is to check the Q feature of C or the Case-assigning feature of T.

To see again how this definition works, consider the intermediate structure from (19b), shown here as (27).

(27)
$[_{TP}$ a man$_i$ $[_{T'}$ to be $[_{SC}$ t$_i$ in the room]]]

The chain (*a man*, t) is incomplete, since the DP *a man* has raised to Spec T and has checked the EPP feature of T but still possesses an unchecked Case feature. The fact that DP possesses this feature makes it the preferred candidate for any further movement operation satisfying Last Resort and Minimality.

Now consider the operation of merging *there* that leads to the structure in (24). This operation is blocked by the movement operation that copies *a man* and raises it to the matrix Spec T, by the principle in (25). Note that this principle is purely local, since the information needed to decide between two operations OP_1 and OP_2 applying to Σ is available in Σ. Let us now see how this principle works with the sentences in (9), repeated here as (28).

(28)
a. *Mary believes to be a man in the room.
b. Mary believes a man to be in the room.

An intermediate structure common to both of these sentences is shown in (29).

(29)
$[_{T'}$ to be $[_{SC}$ a man in the room]]

At this point, raising of *a man* (Copy + Merge) would satisfy Last Resort, so it is allowed. Other economical options would include inserting *Mary* (Copy from the lexicon, plus Merge). However, this operation would eventually lead to an uninterpretable structure, so there is no need to pursue it. After raising of *a man*, we have the structure shown in (30).

(30)
[$_{TP}$ a man$_i$ [$_{T'}$ to be [$_{SC}$ t$_i$ in the room]]]

After forming this structure, the matrix verb is merged with (30) to form the structure shown in (31).

(31)
[$_{V'}$ believes [$_{TP}$ a man$_i$ [$_{T'}$ to be [$_{SC}$ t$_i$ in the room]]]]

The verb *believe* has an external argument in English, and that argument must be introduced at this point in the derivation. This yields (32).

(32)
[$_{VP}$ Mary [$_{V'}$ believes [$_{TP}$ a man$_i$ [$_{T'}$ to be [$_{SC}$ t$_i$ in the room]]]]]

After merging in the matrix T, we have the structure shown in (33).

(33)
[$_{T'}$ T [$_{VP}$ Mary [$_{V'}$ believes [$_{TP}$ a man$_i$ [$_{T'}$ to be [$_{SC}$ t$_i$ in the room]]]]]]

At this point in the derivation there are two possibilities. First, we could raise *Mary*, satisfying Last Resort, since *Mary* would check the Case and EPP feature of the matrix T. Second, we could raise *a man*, satisfying Last Resort, since *a man* would check the Case and the EPP feature of the matrix T.

It would seem that the chain-formation principle in (25) would favor raising *a man* to the specifier of the matrix T. However, raising *a man* would violate Minimality, since there is a closer DP *Mary* that can raise to Spec TP. Therefore, the chain-formation principle is not applicable, and the only possible continuation is moving *Mary* to Spec T as illustrated in (34).

(34)
[$_{TP}$ Mary$_k$ [$_{T'}$ T [$_{VP}$ t$_k$ [$_{V'}$ believes [$_{TP}$ a man$_i$ [$_{T'}$ to be [$_{SC}$ t$_i$ in the room]]]]]]]

After this point, the derivation continues to Spell-Out. After Spell-Out, in the derivation to LF, the Case features of the DP *a man* are raised to a Agr$_O$ or Tr (depending on the theory) to be checked.

Though postulating a chain-formation principle is not strictly minimalist, it is justifiable for the following reasons: First, there is really no alternative given our adoption of local economy and rejection of the Numeration. Second, the notion of chain is needed independent of this analysis, since at LF θ-roles are assigned to chains. Third, all the chain-formation principles seem to revolve around the requirement that the syntactic derivation avoid an incomplete chain.

6.2.1   An Alternative

Poole (1995) presents a different treatment of the expletive sentences that is also local. The problem with Poole's treatment is that it relies on the Numeration, which has been eliminated from the theory. Poole postulates the following economy condition:

(35)   *Total Checking Principle*
The most economical operation is one where an element moves to, or is inserted into, a position where all of the formal features it bears enter into a checking relation.

Poole (1995) takes "checking relation" to mean "asymmetric checking relation" in the sense of chapter 4. Given this principle, consider again these expletive sentences:

(36)
a.   There seems to be a man in the room.
b.   *There seems a man to be in the room.

Once again, consider the following structure, which is a common point in the derivation of both of the sentences in (36):

(37)
[$_{T'}$ to be [$_{SC}$ a man in the room]]

At this point in the derivation, there are two options for satisfying the EPP feature of T. First, we could raise *a man* into Spec T. This would result in the D feature of *a man* entering into a checking relation with the EPP feature of T. (Note that the Case and the ϕ-features of DP do not enter any checking relations with the embedded T. Second, we could insert *there*, which would result in the D feature of *there* entering a checking relation with the EPP feature of the embedded T.) Since (according to Poole) *there* does not bear either Case or ϕ-features, the only feature of *there* (and hence all of the features) has entered into a checking relation. Therefore, by the proposed economy condition (35), insertion of *there* is more economical.[8] This yields the structure shown in (38).

(38)
[$_{TP}$ there [$_{T'}$ to be [$_{SC}$ a man in the room]]

After merging (38) with the matrix verb and T and raising *there*, we obtain the sentence in (36a), the derivation leading to the sentence in (36b) having been blocked.

While Poole's analysis is locally defined (since the decision between inserting *there* and raising *a man* at the structure (37) is made purely on the basis of information available at that structure), this analysis makes crucial use of the Numeration. If at the step (37) there were no Numeration, it would be perfectly acceptable to raise *a man*, since no comparison could be made with inserting *there*. Since there is no Numeration in my theory, Poole's approach must be rejected.

Poole's approach highlights the fact that the Numeration, aside from being essential for theories having global economy, may be used in theories having local economy.

6.3   Conclusion

This chapter has been somewhat more speculative than the other chapters, and had as its main purpose to highlight the conflict between Procrastinate and local economy. We saw how Chomsky's (1993) analysis of verb movement can be modified by modifying the theory of features and eliminating the use of Procrastinate. Finally, we saw how adding a condition on chain formation allows us to analyze expletive constructions without the use of Procrastinate.

Chapter 7
Summary

I began this book with minimalist assumptions concerning the nature of linguistic knowledge. In the minimal theory of linguistic competence, there are two interface levels (PF and LF) and the lexicon. A natural way to relate these components is through a derivation.

In the theory of this book, the operations Merge, Move (= Copy + Merge), and Delete are permissible in a derivation. The goal of the book was to show that all economy conditions on derivations are local.

Concretely, the two economy conditions that play the largest roles in syntax are Last Resort and Minimality. Last Resort, stated below as (1), is used to decide whether a particular operation applies. If the operation results in the satisfaction of one of a limited range of syntactic properties, the operation may apply.

(1) *Last Resort*
An operation OP involving α may apply only if some property of α is satisfied.

Minimality, stated as (2), chooses the smallest among a set of possible operations. In principle, any dimension that allows a comparison (length or number) may be used to determine the smallest operation.

(2) *Minimality*
An operation OP (satisfying Last Resort) may apply only if there is no smaller operation OP′ (satisfying Last Resort).

This approach rules out other global economy conditions, including the Shortest Derivation Requirement (chapter 1) and Procrastinate. Procrastinate is ruled out because it selects the most optimal derivation among the set of convergent derivations, thus rendering global the decision as to whether an operation is part of the optimal derivation.

The notion of convergence (and the principle of Full Interpretation on which it rests) plays a smaller role in a theory with local economy. In the global theory, convergence plays an important role in determining the reference set for the

economy conditions, and therefore in determining which derivation turns out
to be optimal. In the local theory, if a derivation is nonconvergent (for example, some uninterpretable feature is not checked), the LF and the PF are judged
as unacceptable but there are no further consequences. Nonconvergence is just
one of the many ways in which a derivation may lead to an unacceptable (LF,
PF) pair. Other ways include lack of a semantic interpretation and violation of
a local economy condition.

Locative inversion and quotative inversion supply concrete evidence that
global economy is too strong. Consider (3) and (4).

(3)
a. Down the hill rolled John.
b. John rolled down the hill.

(4)
a. "I am so happy," Mary thought.
b. "I am so happy," thought Mary.

In each of these cases, the inverted derivation involves one more step than the
non-inverted derivation. Therefore, the Shortest Derivation Requirement would
block the inverted derivation. Local economy, based on Minimality and Last
Resort, allows both derivations.

Local economy suggests a different perspective on many aspects of phrase
structure. Binary branching can be viewed as the result of Minimality's applying to Merge. In addition, a natural interpretation of Last Resort's applying to
Merge limits Merge to applying when it satisfies the Integration property. The
strict cycle, which has been analyzed in terms of global economy by several
authors, turns out to be deducible from the independently needed Linear
Correspondence Axiom (Kayne 1994).

Last Resort as a local economy condition necessitates a view in which feature checking may be asymmetric. Asymmetric feature checking yields a natural account of ECM and successive cyclicity. In addition, the ban on improper
movement follows from Last Resort.

One surprising consequence of the local economy perspective is that it necessitates the formulation of a number of chain-formation principles. These
principles all have the property that they force the avoidance of incomplete
chains. From the general perspective of local economy, the status of these chain-
formation principles and the very notion of chain are among the most important research issues.

Notes

Chapter 1

1. Brody (1995) has argued extensively, and in an interesting way, against a derivational theory of grammar. Since the economy approach is based on a derivational theory of grammar, Brody's arguments are relevant to this book. Unfortunately, Brody's book appeared too late for me to give detailed consideration to the arguments. I hope that my analyses will further sharpen the derivational theory of grammar, so that a comparison with Brody's theory will become possible.

2. It is easy to see that this approach allows movement of a constituent across phrase structures in S. (See Bobaljik 1995 for a different formalism that has the same effect; see chapter 4 below for discussion.) In chapter 4, I will propose that lexical insertion amounts to movement of a lexical item out of the lexicon.

3. Perhaps it need not be stipulated that Move forms a chain. If no chain is formed, the resulting copy would behave for all purposes as if formed by pure Merge and lexical insertion.

4. Here D is the derivation up to Σ.

5. This definition is not an economy condition; rather, it forces economy conditions to be defined locally. More generally, this definition limits all conditions on operations to be defined locally. The definition says "an optimal derivation," since in the usual case there will be many possible operations at a given point in the derivation that satisfy local economy.

6. I use the word 'information' in a broad sense to include at least the unchecked features and the dominance relations that exist. The question is really what types of information a syntactic operation such as Move or Merge may be sensitive to.

7. In the discussion of locative inversion in section 2.6 and quotative inversion in chapter 3, I will assume that the reference set is determined by the Numeration. This will make my argument against global economy simpler.

8. These terms are defined in chapter 2 below.

9. Ura (1995) also comes to the conclusion that economy operations are not limited to selecting among convergent derivations.

10. See, for example, Chomsky 1986: 30. Consider the following alternative to counting for implementing the Shortest Derivation Requirement: form the set of operations in D_1 {OP_1, OP_2, OP_3), then form the set of operations in derivation D_2 {OP'_1, OP'_2, OP'_3, OP'_4}. Now match up the first members in each set, and eliminate them from D_1 and D_2. Repeat this process for the second members, and continue until there are no more matches left to be made. Whichever derivation ends up with an operation left is the longest. Even this alternative to counting does not seem to necessary in other parts of the grammar, and so it should be excluded for the same reasons counting is.

11. A natural generalization of (3) might be to restrict the evaluation of whether a predicate P holds of Σ to information in Σ. This would exclude the definition of A-position as a potential θ-position. Evaluating whether position X is an A-position would necessitate finding another verb (and therefore a different Σ), and seeing if X is a θ-position with respect to that verb. Similarly, it seems that OT phonology/syntax would be ruled out by this generalization of (3). Evaluating whether Σ is "optimal" involves a comparison to Σ'. Whether OT could be reformulated to make it consistent with this kind of locality is not clear. On a general note, any use of the word 'potential' in a syntactic condition would give rise to similar considerations.

12. The Shortest Derivation Requirement is based on Chomsky 1991, Chomsky 1993, Collins 1994a, and Epstein 1992.

13. This discussion does not address the difficult question of how to account for the impossibility of extracting from subjects in the minimalist framework. See Takahashi 1994 for a possible analysis.

14. I will not go into this analysis any further; the interested reader is referred to Kitahara 1995.

15. Ura (1995: 249) also gives a global analysis, in the sense of (3).

16. The globality of this analysis was independently noticed by Chomsky (1995: 328).

17. In addition to the cases of global economy that I will analyze in this book, the following are examples of global economy: Oka's (1993) use of Fewest Steps in accounting for superiority violations, Kawashima's (1994) use of Shortest Move in deriving the nonscramblability of floated quantifiers (not numerical classifiers) in Japanese, Nakamura's (1994) account of extraction constraints in Tagalog, and Fox's (1995) account of quantifier scope possibilities. Some of these accounts can be recast in local terms, although for reasons of space I will not be able to discuss the analyses in this book.

18. In chapter 6, I will briefly discuss the idea that apparently optional movement may also be the result of a movement taking place before or after Spell-Out. This happens in the case where the feature driving movement is neither strong nor weak (according to the definitions of these terms given in chapter 6).

19. The empirical question of whether a particular operation is optional is usually not so clear. If some feature F may be either strong or weak, the operation resulting in the checking of the feature will appear to be optional. If two derivations (with the same Numeration) have the same number of steps, then global economy allows both derivations. Some cases of apparent optionality may be naturally analyzed in these terms (see, e.g., Chomsky 1991: 431).

Chapter 2

1. This is discussed in chapter 5.

2. See Lasnik 1995 for an alternative analysis.

3. I will return to how the Last Resort fits into this picture in section 2.3.

4. In section 2.2, I will address the question of where the nominative subject moves to at LF. I will give a more detailed analysis of feature checking in locative inversion in section 2.6.

5. See Chomsky 1995 and Ura 1996 for much more discussion.

6. See Bowers 1993 for a related proposal where the external argument is introduced by an independent head. Nishiyama (1996) provides interesting morphological evidence from Japanese for the existence of Tr.

7. Unergative verbs have a Tr that assigns an external θ-role, and may assign accusative Case in certain structures involving cognate objects and resultatives. (See Levin and Rappaport 1995.)

8. This analysis of object shift makes the prediction that a type of locative inversion should exist in Icelandic where a PP could be moved into the outer specifier position of Tr checking the strong D feature of Tr (the Case feature of any object would raise and adjoin to Tr at LF). It does not seem that this exists in Icelandic. This topic as well as the whole topic of locative inversion in Icelandic needs to be looked at in greater detail.

9. There is a long and fruitful literature on object shift based on this assumption, including Chomsky 1993, Deprez 1989, Jonas and Bobaljik 1993, Collins and Thráinsson 1993, and Collins and Thráinsson 1995.

10. I am assuming that a verb such as 'eats' in the sentence "John eats apples" enters the Numeration with two sets of φ-features: subject agreement features and object agreement features. The subject agreement features may be checked by any matching φ-features occupying the checking domain of T, and are spelled out overtly on the verb. The object agreement features may be checked by matching features occupying the checking domain of Tr, and are not spelled out overly on the verb. This tends to suggest that T and Tr are themselves associated with the φ-features (making the multiple-specifier theory even closer to the Agr theory). I will not resolve these issues here, and they are largely irrelevant for the purposes of my analyses.

11. I do not assume that there is distinction between deletion and erasure. (See Chomsky 1995, chapter 4.)

12. In this book, the terms 'interpretable' and 'uninterpretable' cover the same range of features as Chomsky's terms 'Interpretable' and '-Interpretable', respectively.

13. The stronger assumption that F1 and F2 must enter into a checking relation under these conditions is most likely true.

14. What rests on this assumption are sentences where the expletive moves, such as (i) There$_i$ seems t$_i$ to be a man in the garden. If the D feature of the expletive deleted in a checking relation with the EPP feature of the embedded T, the expletive would not be able to undergo any further movement (since further movement would violate Last Resort). This seems to be one point where the distinction between interpretable and uninterpretable breaks down.

15. The original insight that such a condition plays a role in syntax is due to Rizzi (1990).

16. See Oka 1993 for a closely related treatment of locality of movement. The main difference between Oka's system and mine is that Oka makes frequent use of the global economy condition of Fewest Steps.

17. See Ura 1996 for considerable empirical support.

18. Oddly, the notion of length in terms of nodes traversed (Collins 1994a) seems to play no role in Minimality (Ura 1995).

19. I shall return to Ura's analysis in chapter 3.

20. I will leave consideration of how to explain the uniformity condition on Move for further work. Clearly, the logic of my system requires that uniformity either be an independent condition (not part of the definition of Move) or reducible to other conditions (like Last Resort).

21. The relevance of locative inversion for local economy was pointed out to me by Eun Cho.

22. A similar case seems to be Neg-Inversion: (a) At no point did I tell a lie. (b) I told a lie at no point. (c) I did not tell a lie at any point. Although (a) and (b) involve the same lexical choices, (a) is inverted and (b) is not. This inversion would seem to be ruled out by global economy, since inversion requires one more step. The problem is that it is not clear that the Numeration is the same in each case, since (a) may involve a COMP with a strong Spec feature. In locative inversion, both the inverted and the non-inverted derivations satisfy the EPP feature of T, which is strong.

23. See Levin and Rappaport 1994 for a negative evaluation of this assumption. See also Branigan 1993.

24. See Watanabe 1993a for an approach adopting the locality assumptions in Chomsky 1993 that allows for either the DP or PP to move to Spec T.

25. Since movement of the VP to Spec TP would satisfy Last Resort under the text analysis, it may be expected to block movement of the PP by Minimality in (19). However, since the VP dominates (but does not c-command) the PP, it will not block movement of the PP to Spec T (see (20)).

26. Den Dikken and Naess (1993: 306) propose an account of Case checking in locative inversion involving no LF movement. Simplifying somewhat, the post-verbal DP is an indirect sister of T by virtue of the fact that the DP is a sister of the trace of the PP and the PP (after movement) is a sister of T. Unfortunately, this account does not generalize to quotative inversion, where the post-verbal DP and the trace of the quotative operator are definitely not sisters. There are certain restrictions on the type of PP that can undergo locative inversion (described in Levin and Rappaport 1994 and in Den Dikken and Naess 1993) that my account of locative inversion does not explain. For example, a PP describing a location or direction of the theme may undergo locative inversion particularly easily, as in "Into the room walked John." This is part of what Den Dikken and Naess refer to as the "predicativity condition." As far as this condition goes, the account of Den Dikken and Naess is superior to my own.

27. I know of no language in which locative inversion is accompanied by some affix. If the inverted derivation involved an extra affix, it could be claimed that its Numeration

was simply different from that of the non-inverted derivation, and therefore that global economy would be irrelevant.

Chapter 3

1. Although there is little in my analysis that rests on this assumption, some theory-internal evidence for the assumption will be given below.

2. Another possible analysis of (16) that is harder to block is that the adverb occupies an outside specifier position of TrP. If this is allowed, then (16) should be acceptable. Perhaps multiple specifiers of a head H are limited to XPs that have either a feature-checking relation with H or a θ-relation with H. This condition would prohibit an adverb from occupying a specifier position of Tr.

3. Perhaps, as suggested in Collins and Branigan 1995, C has a strong [+quote] feature that drives overt movement to Spec C. Although I do not exclude this possibility, it becomes unimportant on my analysis. However, Howard Lasnik and Hiroyuki Ura have both pointed out to me that there is some reason to believe that the PP in locative inversion undergoes movement to Spec CP. If that is the case, then (assuming quotative and locative inversion to be parallel) we may expect the quote to move to Spec CP.

4. I use the term *operator* mainly to maintain consistency with the terminology of Collins and Branigan 1995. As I noted immediately above, I take no stand on whether the quotative operator eventually moves to Spec C. If it does not, the term *operator* may not be appropriate, as it applies to elements in A′ positions.

5. Quirk et al. (1985: 1022) also note this generalization.

6. In Collins and Branigan 1995 it was argued that overt movement in quotative inversion followed from the fact that the verb must raise to Agr_O in order for the quotative operator to check its Case feature overtly. Since there is no Agr_O in my present account, this analysis is no longer available. If it were to turn out that I need to postulate a strong V feature of T to explain verb movement in quotative inversion, then the inverted derivation and the non-inverted derivation (involving no verb movement) would involve different Numerations. This, in turn, would imply that the analysis of quotative inversion was not relevant to the discussion of local and global economy.

7. The following analysis was influenced by Ura's (1996) analysis of Bantu Inversion.

8. Compare this derivation to my analysis of object shift in section 2.2.

9. Head movement is not represented. The verb has adjoined to Tr overtly, which has adjoined to T overtly.

10. The ordering between (30a) and (30b) is not significant under the theory in this book, nor is ordering between (30c) and (30d).

11. See note 6, however.

12. For brevity I omit the checking relations that are established at each point.

13. The data are from Kilega; see Kinyalolo 1991.

14. As Ura (1996: 250) points out, there is a transitivity constraint on inversion in Bantu.

15. The acceptability of the examples is affected by stressing different words in the sentence (Collins and Thráinsson 1993, 1995).

16. In any theory where the external argument is introduced by a contentful category, such as Tr in my theory, the notion of a VP "shell" (Larson 1988) becomes superfluous.

17. Yiddish, another SVO language, does not have this constraint on scrambling of DPs. This is related to the fact that in other respects scrambling in Yiddish shows A′ properties, as Diesing (1994a) shows.

18. In (50), *bækurnar* "the books" is in the accusative (identical with nominative) and *Maríu* is in the dative (identical with accusative). If *bækurnar* "the books" is put into the dative, the sentence is unacceptable. This shows that switching morphological Case as well as word order does not save the sentence.

19. I assume that the verb has raised to Appl, which has raised to Tr, which has raised to T. Since the position of the verb is not relevant to my explanation of the transitivity constraint, I will omit details the verb's position.

20. One promising example is Eun Cho's (1996) analysis of object shift in Japanese.

Chapter 4

1. I will return to this in section 4.3, where I will show that binary branching does not have to be stipulated.

2. See Chomsky 1994: 396.

3. Unlike Chomsky (1994), I do not assume that the head and the immediate constituents form a complex category of the form {{a,b}, k}, where k is the label. It is not clear at this point whether this difference between my system and Chomsky's has any consequences.

4. This may follow from a suitable generalization of Last Resort, though I do not pursue this generalization here.

5. The definition of adjunction departs from the strictly minimal assumptions about phrase structure embodied in the definitions in (2) and (3). Therefore, this definition can be maintained only if there is unequivocal evidence for adjunction. I will not decide here whether this exists. See chapter 5 for discussion of the relationship between Last Resort and adjunction.

6. *Daughter* can be defined trivially as follows: A is a daughter of B iff A is an element of B. My use of ordered pairs differs from Chomsky's in that he proposes that the ordered pair in an adjunction structure is the label. In my definition of Merge, there is no label.

7. This condition is related to a condition that Chomsky (1994: 393) proposes on the Numeration: the computation does not converge unless all indices in the Numeration are zero. This formulation has a distinctly global flavor, in that it makes reference to convergence. (The relationship between convergence and globality was discussed in chapter 1 above.)

8. It may be possible to derive the fact that Last Resort takes on these specific forms for each type of operation. For example, in the case of Move (Copy + Merge), the relevant property could not be Integration, since one of the affected constituents is already embedded (the moved constituent). See section 4.6.

9. In an earlier version of the present work (Collins 1995), I suggested that Integration follows from LCA. It is possible that Integration reduces to LCA; however, for the reasons given in the text, I will not attempt this reduction here.

10. Even if a transitive verb must always assign accusative case (as the theory of projection based on Tr described in chapter 2 would entail), we would still have to explain why passives and nominalizations have no reflexive reading:

(i)
a. John was hit.
    *John hit himself.
b. John's destruction
    *John's destruction of himself

The empirical generalization that there is no movement into a θ-position is challenged by Lasnik (1995) and Boskovic (1994). (See chapter 2 above for the formulation of Last Resort and chapter 5 below for justification of this formulation.)

11. It may be objected that Integration is not a property of an element X, since it is not included in the set of features of X (phonological, semantic, or formal). It is quite natural that there should be two fundamentally different motivations for Move (features) and Merge (Integration). I will leave further motivation for this distinction to further work.

12. I use "uninterpretable" here to mean that the derivation (18) converges, but the rules of semantic interpretation cannot assign any coherent interpretation to the resulting representation.

13. There may be a number of these simple rules. On the external argument see Collins and Thráinsson 1993 and Collins and Thráinsson 1995.

14. See Kayne 1994, Chomsky 1993, and Chomsky 1994. I simply assume without discussion that all phrase structure is binary branching and that this should be given a syntactic treatment.

15. Where it causes no confusion, I will often write Merge($\{\alpha,\beta,\gamma\}$) as Merge(α,β,γ).

16. A similar issue concerning the generality of economy constraints arises with respect to Last Resort. See the discussion that follows (10); see also note 8 above. Also see section 2.5 of the present book.

17. In a distantly related proposal, Grimshaw (1993) proposes that the projection of functional heads is subject to an economy condition called Min-Proj. Min-Proj is unlike my proposal that Minimality constrains Merge, since Min-Proj may be violated in order to satisfy a higher-ranking constraint. In addition, Min-Proj only restricts the occurrence of functional projections.

18. Strictly, (40) is a branching projection. Still, a branching projection where one of the constituents is the empty set would be difficult to distinguish from a non-branching projection.

19. This section was inspired by Watanabe 1994, page 7 of which has the condition "avoid redefinition of terms as much as possible." In my formulation, redefinition is not allowed at all.

20. There may be empirical reasons to believe that the definition of Merge in (45) is not correct, since countercyclic operations are allowed in certain cases. These include head movement and LF movement, which I discuss in subsections 4.5.1 and 4.5.2.

21. Since no Copy operation has applied in (50vii), there is in fact only one instance of {saw me}, which happens to be contained in two different sets simultaneously. As a purely notational convention, {saw me} is written two times in Σ (50vii).

22. See Collins 1994a and Kitahara 1995 for much discussion of this type of example.

23. See Collins 1994a for the definition of "number of nodes traversed."

24. Similar remarks apply to Kitahara's (1995) analysis, discussed in chapter 1 above.

25. Similar considerations hold for the multiple-specifier theory of clause structure.

26. Although this proposal may seem intuitive for such cases of head movement as clitic movement, noun incorporation, and V-to-I, where the inflectional features of I are checked, it is less clear for V-to-C, where the head adjunction structure plays no morphological role (i.e., no compounding or affixation takes place).

27. The problem may not be significant. If c-command is not stipulated of movement (as I suggested in section 2.5), there is really no reason to expect it to obtain in the case of head movement. Takashi Toyoshima suggested to me that head movement of X to Y may be analyzed as a kind of movement of X to an inner specifier of Y. On this account, head movement would cease to be countercyclic, although other problems would arise.

28. See Collins and Branigan 1995 for an alternative account of quotative inversion that also does not employ an LF cycle.

29. The LF movement analysis of reflexives is a counterexample to the generalization in (61).

30. Bobaljik (1995) suggests that the Copy operation in Move may be eliminated upon careful consideration of the set of terms created at each step in the derivation. However, since Copy will be needed for lexical insertion it is not clear what conceptual advantage Bobaljik's theory has.

31. To make this precise, many more assumptions would have to be clarified—e.g., the nature of movement across phrase structures (subsection 4.5.1).

32. Magui Suñer informs me that some resumptive pronouns in Spanish may be best analyzed as semantically vacuous elements inserted in the branch to PF. The issue of resumptive pronouns (and verbs in predicate cleft constructions) and local economy needs to be looked at in greater detail.

33. It is, however, possible to imagine a theory of local economy that still makes use of the Numeration, as Poole's (1995) analysis (which I will discuss in chapter 6) shows.

34. Chomsky (1995: 294, 377) also employs the Numeration in the following economy condition: (i) α enters the Numeration only if it has an effect on output. This is clearly a very global condition. The decision about whether to enter α in the Numeration depends on information available only at the output levels (PF, LF). Clearly, local economy suggests that an alternative should be looked for. I will not pursue this issue here. See Reinhart 1995 for the notion of Interface Economy, which could be relevant in eliminating (i).

Chapter 5

1. Irrelevant AgrP projections are left out.

2. The definition of Greedier in Collins 1995 is modified from Collins 1994d. (This modification was based on a suggestion of Noam Chomsky.) The statement in Collins 1994d was "Move α raises to a position β only if β is a checking position for a feature belonging to the feature class of an unchecked feature of α." The intent of this definition was to allow asymmetric feature checking. My definition of Last Resort refines and extends the "Myopia" condition of Demuth and Gruber (1994). Lasnik (1995) independently arrives at a similar condition called Enlightened Self Interest.

3. As Chomsky (1995) shows, the theory of asymmetric feature checking extends naturally to account for multiple-subject constructions. (See Ura 1994 and Ura 1996 for extensive discussion of these construction.) Clearly, phenomena such as serial verb constructions also may be accounted for by multiple feature checking (Collins 1993, 1994b, 1994c).

4. It is not clear how the feminine feature in the French *la table* 'the table' contributes to the interpretation of the phrase. Therefore, the distinction between interpretable and uninterpretable features may be more adequately characterized as the distinction between inherent and relational features.

5. Molly Diesing raises the question about languages in which there is some correlation between Case variations and specificity. I leave this question unanswered.

6. See Carstens 1994: 19 for a similar analysis of successive cyclic A-movement under different assumptions about the nature of Case and agreement. Carstens (1994: 38) also notes that Case features are quite different from agreement features as to the number relations they can enter. She calls features such as Case *paired features*.

7. Demuth and Gruber call this the *Basic Projection Sequence* and present arguments to show that it is found universally. Under the assumptions in chapter 4 of Chomsky 1995, where agreement projections are eliminated, it would have to be assumed that the intermediate T projections have agreement features.

8. In section 2.4, I mentioned that Minimality may be given a symmetric interpretation in which intermediate heads with undeleted features may block movement. Under this interpretation, Minimality would force movement to Spec Agr_2.

9. In addition to the multiple agreement found in Bantu compound tenses, it may be possible that a kind of null Case is checked by the word *go* "to" found in control and raising constructions. See Demuth and Gruber 1994 for much discussion of this element.

10. The facts about Ewe pronoun selection are elaborated in Collins 1993 and in Collins 1994a.

11. A similar pattern holds of Hausa auxiliary selection and French stylistic inversion.

12. Direct movement of the *wh*-phrase to the matrix Spec CP in (33) would not violate Minimality (as given in chapter 2), since there is no *wh*-phrase closer to the matrix Spec CP to be moved.

13. See Rizzi 1990: 55 for a discussion of Kinande, which patterns much as Ewe does. Rizzi postulates optional agreement in this case, which would result in a violation of Last Resort under my system.

14. It is not entirely clear what the consequences of this analysis are for the theory of locality of A′-movement presented in Chomsky 1986. In that theory, adjunction to VP allowed an argument to be extracted out of an island, incurring only a mild violation (see also Chomsky and Lasnik 1993). It is my feeling that considerations arising from Last Resort are going to necessitate a rethinking of the entire argument/adjunct asymmetry.

15. See Chomsky 1995: 300 for a view that is consistent with the one adopted below.

16. Ultimately, (41) is a kind of economy condition: Do not form a chain unless you form a complete chain.

17. A more general definition will be given in chapter 6.

18. This definition of incomplete chain relies on the ability of the computational system to verify at LF whether the [+wh] feature of a wh-phrase has entered into a checking relation with the [+wh] feature of a C. This is clearly a nontrivial assumption; in fact, it may be reason to reject the following theory.

19. I assume, following Dayal (1994), that the so-called partial wh-movement in German and Hindi does not in fact involve partial wh-movement.

20. Consider the following example of a multiple question: Who said that what was eaten? Our principle (41) does not rule this out, since what has not entered into a checking relation with a C[+wh].

21. See Fukui 1993 for further discussion of this issue.

22. On p. 99 of Collins 1995 an attempt is made to extend this treatment of improper movement to certain restrictions on clause internal scrambling in Japanese and Yiddish.

23. See Sakai 1994 for a treatment of improper movement in terms of Sakai's "Uniform Sequence Requirement," which is similar to my Chain Formation Principle 3. I thank Akira Watanabe for bringing this reference to my attention.

Chapter 6

1. One problematic case for these definitions is where T has a strong EPP feature and a weak Case feature, and the strong EPP feature enters into a checking relation with the D feature of a DP before Spell-Out. The definitions in (4) imply that the weak Case feature of T may not enter into a checking relation with the Case feature of T unless the Case feature of DP is pure. In this situation, it is not clear that the Case feature of the DP is ever a pure feature, in the sense that the lexical item including the Case feature will never be completely stripped before LF. I leave this as a problematic aspect of my account.

2. Another more exotic possibility is that a feature could be both strong and weak at the same time. This feature would be visible at PF (and therefore must be checked before PF) but can only be checked by a pure feature. This may be another way of characterizing Watanabe's (1992) analysis of Japanese wh-movement, although many questions come to mind.

3. Another problem with Procrastinate is the notion of strength. The basic property of strength is that a feature that is strong causes a derivation to crash at PF. Yet there are other things in a lexical item (LI = {S, F, P}; semantic, formal, and phonological features) that could cause a derivation to crash. If Spell-Out fails to eliminate the semantic features

from a LI, the derivation will crash at PF. Given this consideration, it seems more reasonable to view a strong feature as one that forces the semantic component of a lexical item (say, T) to be visible at PF.

4. See p. 57 of Watanabe 1992 for a related idea.

5. The pattern in (7) seems to be general. Rizzi (1990: 35) shows that a measure phrase may be extracted from an AP, or the measure phrase may pied-pipe the AP (the latter being stylistically marked). This state of affairs is not expected under (6). Incidentally, the data in (7) and the Italian data provide additional support for the conclusion that global economy (i.e., (6)) makes the wrong predictions about optionality. The argument is similar to the one I used in chapters 2 and 3 to reject the Shortest Derivation Requirement on the basis of locative inversion and quotative inversion.

6. These two accounts are very similar, so I treat only Chomsky 1995.

7. Example (26b) should refer to both D and ϕ-features, which can both give rise to incomplete chains.

8. Hiroyuki Ura points out to me that this makes the prediction that in a language where the expletives have ϕ-features (such as French) both of the equivalents of (36a) and (36b) should be allowed.

References

Bobaljik, Jonathan. 1995. In Terms of Merge: Copy and Head Movement. *MIT Working Papers in Linguistics* 27: 41–64.

Bošković, Željko. 1994. D-Structure, Theta-Criterion and Movement into a Theta-Position. *Linguistic Analysis* 24: 247–286.

Bowers, John. 1993. The Syntax of Predication. *Linguistic Inquiry* 24: 591–656.

Branigan, Phil. 1993. Locative Inversion and the Extended Projection Principle. Manuscript, Memorial University of Newfoundland.

Branigan, Phil, and Chris Collins. 1993. Verb Movement and the Quotative Construction in English. *MIT Working Papers in Linguistics* 18: 1–13.

Brody, Michael. 1995. *Lexico-Logical Form: A Radically Minimalist Approach*. MIT Press.

Bures, Anton. 1993. There Is an Argument for an LF Cycle Here. *Chicago Linguistic Society* 28: 14–35.

Cardinaletti, Anna, and Michal Starke. 1994. The Typology of Structural Deficiency. Manuscript, University of Venice and University of Geneva.

Carstens, Vicki. 1994. Deriving Agreement. Manuscript, Cornell University.

Cho, Eun. 1996. A-Scrambling as an Attraction Driven by [+multiple] EPP. Manuscript, Cornell University.

Chomsky, Noam. 1986. *Barriers*. MIT Press.

Chomsky, Noam. 1991. Some Notes on Economy of Derivation and Representation. In *Principles and Parameters in Comparative Grammar*, ed. R. Freidin. MIT Press.

Chomsky, Noam. 1993. A Minimalist Program for Linguistic Theory. In *The View from Building 20*, ed. K. Hale and S. Keyser. MIT Press.

Chomsky, Noam. 1994. Bare Phrase Structure. *MIT Occasional Papers in Linguistics* 5. Also in *Government and Binding Theory and the Minimalist Program*, ed. G. Webelhuth (Blackwell, 1995).

Chomsky, Noam. 1995. *The Minimalist Program*. MIT Press.

Chomsky, Noam, and Howard Lasnik. 1993. Principles and Parameters Theory. In *Syntax: An International Handbook of Contemporary Research*, ed. J. Jacobs et al. Walter de Gruyter.

Chung, Sandra, and James McCloskey. 1987. Government, Barriers, and Small Clauses in Modern Irish. *Linguistic Inquiry* 18: 173–237.

Collins, Chris. 1992. A Note on Verb Second in English. Manuscript, Massachusetts Institute of Technology.

Collins, Chris. 1993. Topics in Ewe Syntax. Doctoral dissertation, Massachusetts Institute of Technology.

Collins, Chris. 1994a. Economy of Derivation and the Generalized Proper Binding Condition. *Linguistic Inquiry* 25: 45–61.

Collins, Chris. 1994b. Argument Sharing in Serial Verb Constructions. Manuscript, Cornell University.

Collins, Chris. 1994c. Serial Verb Constructions and the Theory of Multiple Feature Checking. Manuscript, Cornell University.

Collins, Chris. 1994d. Merge and Greed. Manuscript, Cornell University.

Collins, Chris. 1995. Towards a Theory of Optimal Derivations. *MIT Working Papers in Linguistics* 27: 65–103.

Collins, Chris, and Phil Branigan. 1995. Quotative Inversion. Manuscript, Cornell University and Memorial University of Newfoundland.

Collins, Chris, and Höskuldur Thráinsson. 1993. Object Shift in Double Object Constructions and the Theory of Case. *MIT Working Papers in Linguistics* 19: 131–174.

Collins, Chris, and Höskuldur Thráinsson. 1995. VP Internal Structure and Object Shift in Icelandic. Manuscript, Cornell University and Harvard University.

Dayal, Veneeta Srivastav. 1994. Scope Marking as Indirect Wh-Dependency. *Natural Language Semantics* 2: 137–170.

Demuth, Katherine, and Jeffery Gruber. 1994. Constraining XP Sequences. Manuscript, Brown University and Université du Québec.

Den Dikken, M., and A. Naess. 1993. Case Dependencies: The Case of Predicate Inversion. *Linguistic Review* 10: 303–336.

Déprez, Viviane. 1989. On the Typology of Syntactic Positions and the Nature of Chains. Doctoral dissertation, Massachusetts Institute of Technology.

Diesing, Molly. 1994a. Yiddish VP Order and Leftward Movement in Germanic. Manuscript, Cornell University.

Diesing, Molly. 1994b. Comments on Cardinaletti and Starke: "The Typology of Structural Deficiency," Manuscript, Cornell University.

Epstein, Samuel David. 1992. Derivational Constraints on A'-Chain Formation. *Linguistic Inquiry* 23: 235–259.

Fox, Danny. 1995. Economy and Scopy. Manuscript, Massachusetts Institute of Technology.

Fukui, Noaki. 1993. A Note on Improper Movement. *Linguistic Review* 10: 111–126.

Grimshaw, Jane. 1993. Minimal Projection, Heads and Optimality. Technical Report 4, Rutgers University Center for Cognitive Science.

Hale, Ken, and Samuel Jay Keyser. 1993. On Argument Structure and the Lexical Expression of Syntactic Relations. In *The View from Building 20*, ed. K. Hale and S. Keyser. MIT Press.

Holmberg, Anders. 1986. Word Order and Syntactic Features in the Scandinavian Languages and English. Doctoral dissertation, University of Stockholm.

Jonas, Dianne, and Jonathan D. Bobaljik. 1993. Specs for Subjects: The Role of TP in Icelandic. *MIT Working Papers in Linguistics* 18: 59–98.

Kawashima, Ruriko. 1994. The Structure of Noun Phrases and the Interpretation of Quantificational NPs in Japanese. Doctoral dissertation, Cornell University.

Kayne, Richard. 1994. *The Antisymmetry of Syntax*. MIT Press.

Kinyalolo, Kasangati. 1991. Syntactic Dependencies and the Spec-Head Agreement Hypothesis in Kilega. Doctoral dissertation, University of California, Los Angeles.

Kitahara, Hisatsugu. 1994. Target α: A Unified Theory of Movement and Structure-Building. Doctoral dissertation, Harvard University.

Kitahara, Hisatsugu. 1995. Target α: Deducing Strict Cyclicity from Derivational Economy. *Linguistic Inquiry* 26: 47–77.

Koizumi, Masatoshi. 1993. Object Agreement Phrases and the Split VP Hypothesis. Papers on Case and Agreement II. *MIT Working Papers in Linguistics* 18: 99–148.

Koizumi, Masa. 1994. Layered Specifiers. *Proceedings of the NELS* 24: 255–269.

Kratzer, Angelika. 1994. On External Arguments. Occasional Paper 17, University of Massachusetts, Amherst.

Larson, Richard. 1988. On the Double Object Construction. *Linguistic Inquiry* 19: 335–391.

Lasnik, Howard. 1993. Lectures on Minimalist Syntax. *University of Connecticut Working Papers in Linguistics*, Occasional Papers Issue 1.

Lasnik, Howard. 1995. Last Resort and Attract F. In *Proceedings of FLSM 6*. Indiana University Linguistics Club.

Levin, Beth, and Malka Rappaport Hovav. 1994. *Unaccusativity: At the Syntax–Lexical Semantics Interface*. MIT Press.

Marantz, Alec. 1993. Implications of Asymmetries in Double Object Constructions. In *Theoretical Aspects of Bantu Grammar*, ed. S. Mochombo. CSLI.

May, Robert. 1979. Must Comp-to-Comp Movement be Stipulated? *Linguistic Inquiry* 10: 719–725.

McCawley, James. 1982. Parentheticals and Discontinuous Constituent Structure. *Linguistic Inquiry* 13: 91–106.

McCloskey, James. 1979. *Transformational Syntax and Model Theoretical Semantics*. Reidel.

Müller, Gereon. 1994. Anti-Freezing, Strict Cyclicity and Economy of Derivation. Manuscript, Universität Tübingen.

Nakamura, Masanori. 1994. An Economy Account of Wh-Extraction in Tagalog. In *Proceedings of the Twelfth West Coast Conference on Formal Linguistics*. CLSI.

Nishiyama, Kunio. 1996. Spelling Out Voice: s/r Alternation in Japanese. Manuscript, Cornell University.

Oka, Toshifusa. 1993. Shallowness. *MIT Working Papers in Linguistics* 19: 255–320.

Pollock, Jean-Yves. 1989. Verb Movement, Universal Grammar, and the Structure of IP. *Linguistic Inquiry* 20: 365–424.

Poole, Geoffrey. 1995. Constraints on Local Economy. In *Is the Best Good Enough?* ed. P. Barbosa et al. MIT Press.

Quirk, Randolph, Sidney Greenbaum, Geoffrey Leech, and Jan Svartvik. 1985. *A Comprehensive Grammar of the English Language*. Longman.

Reinhart, Tanya. 1995. Interface Strategies. OTS Working Paper, Utrecht University.

Rizzi, Luigi. 1990. *Relativized Minimality*. MIT Press.

Sakai, Hiromu. 1994. Derivational Economy and Long Distance Scrambling in Japanese. *MIT Working Papers in Linguistics* 24: 295–314.

Sportiche, Dominique. 1988. A Theory of Floating Quantifiers and Its Corollaries for Constituent Structure. *Linguistic Inquiry* 19: 425–449.

Takahashi, Daiko. 1994. Minimality of Movement. Doctoral dissertation, University of Connecticut.

Travis, Lisa. 1984. Parameters and the Effects of Word Order Variation. Doctoral dissertation, Massachusetts Institute of Technology.

Ura, Hiroyuki. 1994. Varieties of Raising and the Feature-Based Bare Phrase Structure Theory. *MIT Occasional Papers in Linguistics*, no. 7.

Ura, Hiroyuki. 1995. Towards a Theory of a "Strictly Derivational" Economy Condition. *MIT Working Papers in Linguistics* 27: 243–267.

Ura, Hiroyuki. 1996. Multiple Feature Checking: A Theory of Grammatical Function Splitting. Doctoral dissertation, Massachusetts Institute of Technology.

Watanabe, Akira. 1992. Wh-in-Situ, Subjacency and Chain Formation. MIT Occasional Paper in Linguistics 2.

Watanabe, Akira. 1993a. Locative Inversion: Where Unaccusativity Meets Minimality. Manuscript, University of Tokyo.

Watanabe, Akira. 1993b. AGR-Based Case Theory and its Interaction with the A-Bar System. Doctoral dissertation, Massachusetts Institute of Technology.

Watanabe, Akira. 1994. A Cross-Linguistic Perspective on Japanese Nominative-Genitive Conversion and its Implications for Japanese Syntax. Manuscript, Kanda University, Tokyo.

Watanabe, Akira. 1995a. The Conceptual Basis of Cyclicity. *MIT Working Papers in Linguistics* 27: 269–291.

Watanabe, Akira. 1995b. Case Absorption and Wh-Agreement. Manuscript, Kanda University of International Studies, Japan.

Index

Adjunction, 37, 64–65, 108
Adverbs, 36–37, 115–116
Affix, applicative, 53–61
AgrP, 16–19, 36, 50–53, 74, 85–86, 88, 96–98, 103–104
Argument, external, 15, 53
Attract, 22, 25–26, 101

Branching, binary, 63, 75–78, 94, 130

Case, 23, 70–71, 74, 78, 88–89, 93. *See also* T; Tr
  and incomplete chains, 124–126
  and interpretability, 21–22
  and Last Resort, 97–104, 112
  in locative inversion, 28–30
  in quotative inversion, 33–34, 40–61
C-command, 26, 67, 83–88
Chain formation, 3, 47, 91–92, 108–114, 123–125, 130
Checking
  domain, 20
  and intermediate adjunction, 108, 114
  and θ-role assignment, 69–73
  of pure features, 117–120
  relation, 20, 28, 95
Convergence, 4–6, 10, 25–26, 29, 46, 68, 71, 78, 129–130
  and pied-piping, 119–120
  and Procrastinate, 6, 116, 121–122
  and uninterpretable features, 21, 100, 112
  and θ-Criterion, 71–73
Copy, 2, 25–26, 90–94, 129

Deletion, 2, 25, 76, 90
  and chain formation, 3, 89, 91–92
  vs. erasure, 101
  and feature checking, 3, 20–22, 100–101, 111
  recoverability of, 101–102
Do-support, 41
Double object constructions, 50–61
D-Structure, 67

Enlightened Self Interest, 139n2
Equidistance, 18, 23–24, 27, 43–44, 54
Ewe, 105–108
Exceptional Case Marking, 73, 89, 96–102, 120–127, 130
Expletives, 14–16, 21–22, 68–69, 73, 80, 89, 93, and Procrastinate, 120–127
Extended Projection Principle, 17, 21, 24, 69–70
  independence from Case, 13, 14, 100
  and Last Resort, 97, 100–102, 104, 109, 112–113
  in locative inversion, 27–30
  and Procrastinate, 121–126
  in quotative inversion, 38–49, 58–61
Extension condition, 8, 81

Feature checking, asymmetric, 20–22, 43–44, 98–108
Floated quantifiers, 33
French, 115–118

Global economy, 4–11, 68–69, 71, 85, 98, 113–114, 129
  and locative inversion, 29–30
  and Procrastinate, 116–127
  and quotative inversion, 45–47, 61
Greed, 6, 96–99, 103

Head, 63–65, 86–88
Head Movement Constraint, 35–36, 64
Heavy NP Shift, 32–33

Icelandic, 16–19, 51–57, 85–86, 115
Insertion, lexical, 65–69, 90–94
  vs. movement, 91–92
Integration, 65–75, 80, 91, 94, 122–123, 130
Interleaving, 109
Interpretability, 5, 20–22, 28–29, 44, 99–105
Inversion. *See* Kilega; Locative inversion; Quotative inversion